KU-112-431

© 1991 Verlag Lutz Garnies, D-8011 Neukeferloh/Munich
1992: 2nd revised edition
Grafic-Design, Textconception and Realization: Löhr & Partner, Munich
Typesetting: Eder & Poehlmann, Neukeferloh/Munich
Colour-seperations: OK-Meyer, Munich
Printing and binding: Oldenbourg, Munich

ISBN 3-926163-08-9

5
From Agriculture
to Industry

6
An Economic Area
with a Future

Appendix

1

Geography

n Bavaria . . .
. . . tradition and progress go hand in hand.
. . . unmistakebly
. . . one of the oldest states in Europe
. . . one of the most modern states in Europe
. . . one of the high-tech centres in Germany and Europe
. . . a region for which experts predict a marvellous future

Bayern

Bavaria lies . . .
. . . between a latitude of 47°16′ and 50°34′ north and
   a longitude of 85°8′ and 13°50′ east, that is
. . . in the middle of Europe
. . . between Bayreuth and Bamberg
. . . between bytes and Barock
. . . at the point where people live in the present,
   care for the past and work on the future.
. . . just in the right place!

1 *Panoramic view
   from the top of the
   Zugspitze*

2 *The Basilica in
   Ottobeuren*

1

2

1

1 *Königsee*

2 *View of Geroldsee
to the Zugspitze
(Bavaria)*

3 *Ammersee*

4 *Burghausen*

Bayern

2
3

4

11

When Bishop Arbeo of Freising died in 783 he left behind an impressive description of the beauty and natural riches of Bavaria:

"It was beautiful to look at, full of groves and laden with wine. It possessed an abundance of iron and was plentiful in gold and silver. Its men were tall, strong, virtuous and of high moral standing.

The soil was fertile bringing forth crops in plenty and every type of cattle you could imagine seemed to cover the countryside. Honey and bees were truly in great abundance.

The lakes and rivers were full of fish, the land was irrigated by clear springs and brooks and contained as much salt as was required. The low mountain regions were rich in fruit and grazing land of lush grass. The wooded mountain areas were populated with wild animals, the undergrowth with deer, elk, oxen, roe-deer, ibex and game of every description.

With a total area of 70,553 square kilometres Bavaria is Germany's largest state-as big as Ireland and bigger than Switzerland or Denmark. Within its borders there are 11 million inhabitants – more than in Portugal, Belgium, Greece, Austria or Sweden.

If one took size, population or even economic potential as a yardstick, Bavaria could quite easily be an independent state with an important position within Europe.

1 *The old King Ludwig Donau-Main Canal*

2 *Winter scene in Upper Bavaria*

3 *Autumn in Jura, Upper Bavaria*

3

Bayern

Bavaria's blue and white sky covers a charming and varied countryside, attracting millions of tourists every year. Four naturally-formed areas dominate the state.

– the Bavarian Alps with their fascinating views across mountains mostly over 2,000 metres high including the Zugspitze which, at 2,964 metres, is Germany's highest mountain.

15

– the Alpine Lowlands stretch from the Alps to the Danube. Countless lakes are scattered across the lush, lightly undulating countryside offering a

1 *Taubensee with the mountains Watzmann and Hochkalter*

2 *The top of the Zugspitze*

3 *West Allgäu – the village of Simmerberg*

multitude of possibilities for sport and recreation.

– the East Bavarian Central Mountain Range which stretches from Passau to Regensburg and through to the Czechoslovakian border. Hill-side woods, lakes and towering

1 *A stork's nest.*

2 *A scene from the forests of the Upper Palatinate.*

3 *A museum ship in Regensburg.*

mountains dominate this rugged landscape. Here you can find Germany's first national park, the Bavarian Forest National Park.

– the Swabian-Franconian area with its terraced landscape is a north Bavarian plateau between the East Bavarian Central Mountain Range and the Danube. The rivers Spessart and Rhön form the natural borders to Hesse.

Bayern

4 *Passau-where the Inn and the Danube meet.*

5 *The Bavarian Forest with Stei-nernes Meer near Dreisessel.*

6 *The Weltenburg Monastery.*

7 *The ruins of the Weißenstein Castle at Regen, with the Bavarian Forest and a view of the Arber.*

1 *Munich with a view of
Ludwigstrasse.*

Bayern

Seven regional districts form the administrative backbone of Bavaria. Upper and Lower Bavaria, Swabia, the Upper Palatinate, Upper Lower and Central Franconia.

Far-reaching economic and structural policies set the course early on for a balanced development of the seven regions. Even if the economic and political heart of Bavaria is Munich and the surrounding areas, the other regions have kept their cultural identity and built on their specific economic strengths. That is especially the case in Lower Bavaria and the Upper Palatinate which for many years suffered from bordering on the "Iron Curtain". The traditional trade routes to the East, and in particular to Bohemia, were suddenly closed. As a place to do business the area was, at least initially, unattractive. And yet with a concentrated effort to promote these regions the disadvantages could – at least partially – be made good. Upper Bavaria's capital Munich is also Bavaria's capital. This is where Bavaria's economic centre is to be found, a high-tech metropolis with a wide range of businesses and enterprises. The cultural opportunities are large and varied as are those for sport and recreation which have all added to the attractiveness of the region.

From a geographical point of view Upper Bavaria encompasses the Bavarian Alps, the Alpine Lowlands and the Danube Valley near Ingolstadt. The administrative region of Lower Bavaria has Landshut as its capital and includes the north-east of the German Alpine Lowlands, the Danube Valley between Straubing and Passau as well as a large part of the Bavarian Forest. The latter, with its unspoilt woods, its mountains and almost untouched natural beauty, remains a great attraction for tourists. Many traditional handicrafts are fostered here, above all glass painting and wood carving. More than anything else, however, Lower Bavaria is a superb example of how a successful structural policy can be implemented. The Munich II airport, situated nearby, should add to the attractive-

3

19

2

2 *Winter on the Arber in the Bavarian Forest.*

3 *The Bavarian Forest National Park is rich in flora and fauna.*

4 *Wood carvers from Oberammergau.*

4

ness of the region still further. Upper Palatinate has in Regensburg the royal house of Thurn and Taxis and one of Germany's largest private fortunes as well as the descendants of the founders of the 500-year-old German postal system within its borders. From a geographical point of view Upper Palatinate comprises the catchment area around the Naab as well as the basin around Amberg. Iron, glass and pottery traditionally dominate the industrial face of the region. The consolidated development of the road and rail network coupled with clear structural policies and a forward-looking approach to attracting new businesses to settle there have enabled Upper Palatinate to make substantial progress as a region over the years.

The administrative region of Swabia includes the Allgäu Alps, the Alpine Lowlands, the flatland around the Danube and the Swabian Alb. Its capital is Augsburg which, besides Munich, Nuremberg and Ingolstadt, is another important centre of industry and commerce in Bavaria. Over 600 years ago the Fuggers, a house of traders, resided here, gaining an importance in trade and finance between the fourteenth and sixteenth centuries comparable to that of the Medicis in Florence. Augsburg has to be grateful to the Fuggers for the establishment of the oldest housing scheme in the world in 1514 – which is still in use today by the way.

1 *Regensburg Cathedral.*

Central Franconia is, after Munich, the most important economic region in Bavaria. In the conurbations Nuremberg, Erlangen and Fürth well-known companies like Schoeller, Grundig or the largest mail order firm in Germany Quelle GmbH have their headquarters. Electrical and mechanical engineering dominate the industrial landscape here as do the service industries. The Federal Institute for Employment is also a significant employer in the region.

Lower Franconia is famous for its wine and has in Würzburg not only one of the leading Bavarian universities but also a first-class centre for the service industries. Schweinfurt is the mecca of the anti-friction bearing industry and one of the most dynamic economic areas in Bavaria. An industrial landscape representing a variety of economic interests has formed also around Aschaffenburg on the border to Hesse. As one of the oldest industrial areas in Bavaria Upper Franconia can boast an impressive range of businesses and enterprises even

UNTERFRANKEN
Würzburg

OBERFRANKEN
Bayreuth

Ansbach

MITTEL-
FRANKEN

OBERPFALZ
Regensburg

NIEDERBAYERN
Landshut

Augsburg

SCHWABEN

München

OBERBAYERN

today. It is distinguished by a large number of industrial sites such as Hof, Coburg and Selb/ Wundsiedel. For a long time at a disadvantage due to its position along increase in economic significance as a result of German reunification.

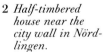

2 *Half-timbered house near the city wall in Nörd-lingen.*

3 *Viniculture in Franconia.*

4 *Oberstdorf with the Haupt-kamm in the background.*

5 *Nuremberg Harbour.*

Bayern

1284
MITTEL-
PUNKT
1985
EUROPAS

C.R. OPER
ASTR TRIG
PRO
MENS GRAD
MED EUROP
1865

ear the small village of Waldsasssen in Upper Palatinate, not far from today's German-Czechoslovakian border, Napoleon is said to have laid a memorial stone in 1805. Exactly on this spot – so they say – the French Emperor saw the geographical centre of the West, the "middle of Europe".

The fact is that at the beginning of the nineteenth century officers of Napoleon in the engineeering corps carried out surveying work in the region making use of a natural landmark – a piece of stone – which today is called the "Napoleon Stone".

For a long time this stone could only be a "middle" in a geographical sense. For centuries it marked the edge of the western world as it looked over to the "Iron Curtain" which divided Europe into two blocks.

And yet with the sweeping political changes of recent times this landmark has taken on its original symbolism again. Today it stands for Bavaria's central position in an open Europe. With the opening of the borders to Czechoslovakia and the reunification of Germany, Bavaria has adopted its traditional role at the centre of European trade and commerce. Once again it can develop centuries-old political and economic ties with the East.

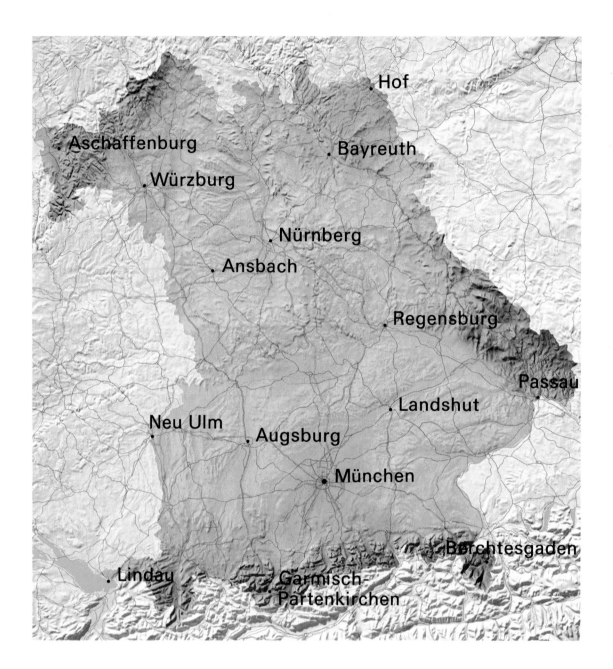

Hof

Aschaffenburg

Bayreuth

Würzburg

Nürnberg

Ansbach

Regensburg

Passau

Landshut

Neu Ulm

Augsburg

München

Berchtesgaden

Lindau

Garmisch-
Partenkirchen

Bayern

From the Alps to the Frankenwald:
Relief map of Bavaria; cross-section from North to South.

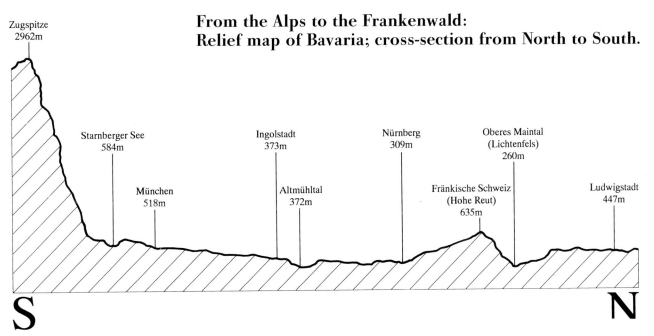

Zugspitze
2962m

Starnberger See
584m

München
518m

Ingolstadt
373m

Altmühltal
372m

Nürnberg
309m

Oberes Maintal
(Lichtenfels)
260m

Fränkische Schweiz
(Hohe Reut)
635m

Ludwigstadt
447m

S

N

1 *A spectacular research project. The drilling point in Windischeschenbach which will enable scientists to make new insights into the structure of the Earth's crust.*

Bavaria's central position predestined it to be a point of intersection for a pan-European economy whose dimensions are impossible to estimate at the moment. As east European nations liberate themselves and adapt to the forces of a social market economy, the exchange of goods with the West is likely to increase rapidly. Bavaria, with its good contacts to the East, is the number one country for through traffic.

A glance at the map will show that Bavaria really does lie in the heart of Europe. It can offer good connections to the most important international cities. London, Paris, Zurich, Milan, Rome, Vienna, Prague or Budapest can all be reached within one or two hours by plane. The extensive motorway network is another plus. Of great importance when transporting freight is the fact that the international railway network also covers large areas of Bavaria.

Works on the Rhein-Main-Danube canal is still in progress. When it is finished the transport system in Bavaria will be even more attractive having one single route for ships to the Black Sea.

Even today Regensburg and many other Bavarian cities are joined to the canal and therefore have harbours which are directly linked to the Black Sea. The new airport Munich II, 30 kilometres from Munich near Erding, will be ready on time for the opening of Europe. With two runways 4,000 metres in length, and an estimated number of passengers reaching 12 million a year, the new airport will mark a new era for Bavaria. The volume of traffic will amount to 250,000 tonnes a year and 10,000 people will be employed to ensure a smooth- running operation both on the ground and in the air.

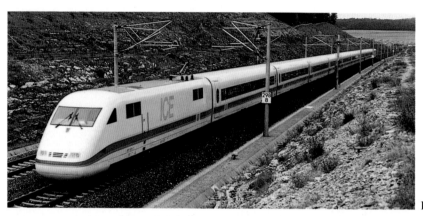

1

2

1 *The high-speed ICE train of the German National Railways.*

2 *Linked to the Black Sea. Regensburg Harbour.*

Within a very short time Munich II is likely to become one of the most significant airports in Europe. Even during the construction phase it was a magnet for a large group of investors, above all for those operating internationally. The new airport has been incorporated into a well thought-out transport system which will ensure that car and rail travellers will be able to reach it easily. Thanks to a direct connection to the Munich train network, the journey from Munich's main station to the airport will take only 30 minutes. A great deal of attention was paid to the environment during the planning and construction phases. To reduce all unavoidable damage to a minimum, a whole set of measures was decided on which went from

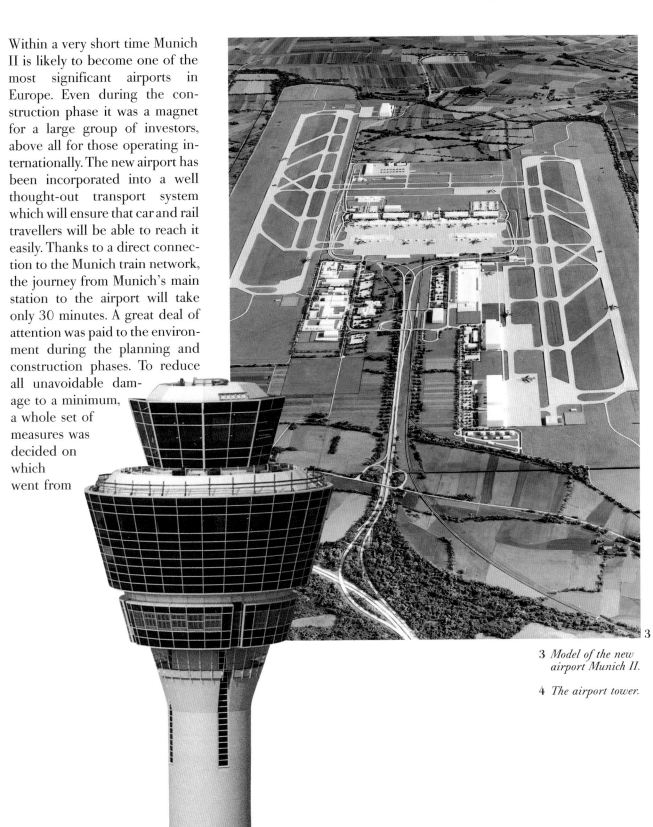

3

3 *Model of the new airport Munich II.*

4 *The airport tower.*

4

maintaining numerous green areas to securing a nature reserve near the airport, to the cleaning of the airport sewage and a completely new microbiological process whereby the poisonous remains from deiceing agents can be turned into harmless substances.

Near the airport "Amadeus", one

1 Partners in transporting people and freight: road ...

2 ... and rail.

3 The railway network in Bavaria.

4 Almost 300 staff control trips around the globe. The computer centre Amadeus near the new airport Munich II.

Bayern

3

4

of the biggest computer centres in the world, is now in operation. Nearly 300 staff in this Pentagon-like building control the national and international reservations of airline and travel companies. The choice of Erding for this facility, with investments reaching several hundred million DM, illustrates the immense significance of the new airport.

2

The People and
their Country

Bayern

cessful economically as well: they claim always to have maintained the balance between being modern and traditional: with all their efficiency and industry the Bavarians represent the outpost of a Mediterranean lifestyle in a desolate north: perhaps the proximity to Italy has given them the characteristics of being happy and relaxed – and all this interspersed with baroque elements and a good portion of realism.

avarians are different. So they say. The Bavarians like to say so themselves. The reason is to be found in their well developed sense for cultural heritage and an independent identity. Let's make it quite clear. The knowledge that they are something special is widespread: they are one of the oldest states in Europe, for example, and one of the most suc-

hat have you heard about the Bavarians? It doesn't matter. Forget it! It's probably a prejudice, founded on ignorance, resentment or false information. The fact is Bavarians are charming people, warm and kind. Open, of course, and tolerant. A mind of their own? Certainly. Now and then passionate, too. Above all they do not take themselves as seriously as it might seem. A Bavarian can certainly laugh about himself – but not everybody needs to know that.

The corner-stone of Bavarian mentality is to be found in the much-quoted "Liberalitas bavariae" whose motto "live and let live" bears witness to Bavarian tolerance. For many years now anything or anyone original has flourished on Bavarian soil as has a person with a mind of his own who is prepared to accept others who think likewise. Of course, this sort of attitude can only find roots in a self-confidence which is rarely attacked by feelings of doubt. And, by the way, there are no "Bavarians". There are Old Bavarians, the inhabitants of Upper Bavaria, Lower Bavaria and Upper Palatinate.

They are known to have artistic tendencies and to be open – at least until the opposite can be proved. The Franconians, they say, like order in their lives. Or to put it in a friendlier way: they have organisational talents, just as much as they are happy people and intellectually flexible. The Swabians, it is said, rarely let their

joy of life flow over into wastefulness or enthusiasm. It could be that this verdict is as much their fault as anybody else's.

For reasons of venerableness the so-called "fourth tribe" in Bavaria cannot be included with the other three ones. The 2 million or so people driven out of their homes during the World War II, above all the Sudeten Germans, now find themselves under the patronage of the Free State. They brought new life and technical and manual skills into Bavaria and played a significant part in the reconstruction work in the

post-war years. Today they are completely at home here.

Religion had and continues to have a great effect on the inner life of Bavarians. The constitution pledges the state to neutrality in religious matters. Almost 70 per cent of the population are Catholic and 26 per cent Protestant. The dominant role of the Catholic faith cannot be measured in terms of this superiority in figures, however. It is much more a dominant force for countless monuments, in local customs and festivals and not least in people's conduct in their everyday lives.

Tradition – it's clothing that's too tight, uncomfortable, old-fashioned, yet warm providing a sense of security and orientation. More than other German states Bavaria fosters its cultural heritage.

The unforgettable "father of the Bavarians", Franz Josef Strauß, made the point like this:

"In order to know where they are and where they are going, people have to know where they have come from. This goes for history in general just as much as it does for our cultural and spiritual roots."

An important aspect of this awareness can be found in the protection of monuments. Maintaining what is art-historically valuable, or preserving testimonies of past pomp and significance has a long tradition. But the idea that we should protect everything which belonged to a past epoch is relatively new. This means protecting all those unspectacular things, houses or everyday objects, which people found important at the time. In this sense groups of buildings, farms, complete villages or suburbs have now become the subject of attention.

1 *Herr Geiger from the sculpture workshop of the Bavarian castles management section.*

2 *Supported by the Hypo bank. The renovated Wastl farm in Upper Bavaria.*

3 *These well looked after facades are typical of Bavarian cities.*

4 *A detail of the Abstreiter family's farmhouse, winner of the Hypo Monument Prize 1988.*

Bayern

6

5

5 *Hypo Monument Prize 1990 for detailed work on the Blue Castle in Obernzerrn. The staircase on the righthand has been painted on the wall.*

6/7 *Before and after. The house at Mühlgasse 11. Hypo Monument Prize 1989.*

7

1-4 *Renovation work on the Pilgrimage Church Wies in Upper Bavaria.*

Bavarian villages – nestling between hills, pastures, rivers and fields – are inseparable from their inhabitants. A rural landscape without villages which have evolved over the years is unthinkable. The church, the pub, the butchers, the bakery and of course the farms dominated the image of the village in the past – and continue to do so today.

In the area of monument protection Bavaria is playing a leading role. As long ago as 1835, under King Ludwig 1, Bavaria, as the first German state, founded an inspection general to take care of the state's monuments.

A new era in monument protection began in 1973 with the introduction of the Monument Protection Law, which not only in Germany but throughout Europe was considered exemplary. At the same time a Council for State Monuments was established as a permanent institution.

An important step was exploiting the knowledge of a team of specialists to draw up a list of buildings in need of protection. At present this list contains the names of 110,000 buildings, nearly 90,000 ensembles and 10,000 archaeological sites. It includes castles, churches, monasteries,

2

3

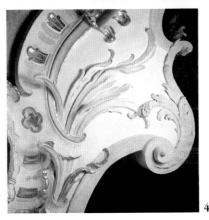

4

farms, city walls and towers, cemetries, technical facilities and a lot more.

Every year over 60 million DM are spent by the Bavarian government on the upkeeping of monuments. Another 70 million DM are provided by Bavaria in the form of grants and loans for the maintenance of buildings and ensembles which are not owned by the Free State.

The administrative offices of the state gardens, castles and lakes, which can be found in the appropriate environment of the Nymphenburg Castle and the Office for Monument Preservation in Bavaria, which is situated in the "Alte Münze" in the old part of Munich, look after this historical heritage with care and attention. An important side-effect of all these efforts: through the preservation of monuments many craftsmen have been able to work in professions which otherwise would have long since died out, such as ornamental plasterers or wrought iron artworkers.

1

It is not just the superficial facades of past epochs which have been preserved. Present-day customs are also testimonies of the Bavarian sense of identity. Countless people, organised in groups, ensure that folk dancing and folk costumes, along with their corresponding customs and practices, are not forgotten. At festivals and traditional occasions they spend a great deal of time and money to present their art with all the energy and enthusiasm they have. The "Leonhardifahrt" in Bad Tölz, for example, is not at all for tourists, but a custom which the people can be proud of.

By the way. If you wear traditional Bavarian suits or dresses you are always correctly dressed for society life in Munich!

2

In the mainly rural areas of Bavaria a traditional sort of custom has been kept alive which is neither a tourist attraction nor an out-of-date clinging to the past. It is much more a lively and for the most part religiously significant aspect of the culture of everyday life and festivals.

1 *Alpine horn
   players.*

2 *The procession at
   the Oktoberfest.*

3 *Roadside shrine
   in Franconia.*

4 *Traditional pro-
   cession costumes
   at the Oktoberfest.*

5 *Bavarian brass
   music corps at the
   Oktoberfest proces-
   sion on Odeons-
   platz.*

Bayern

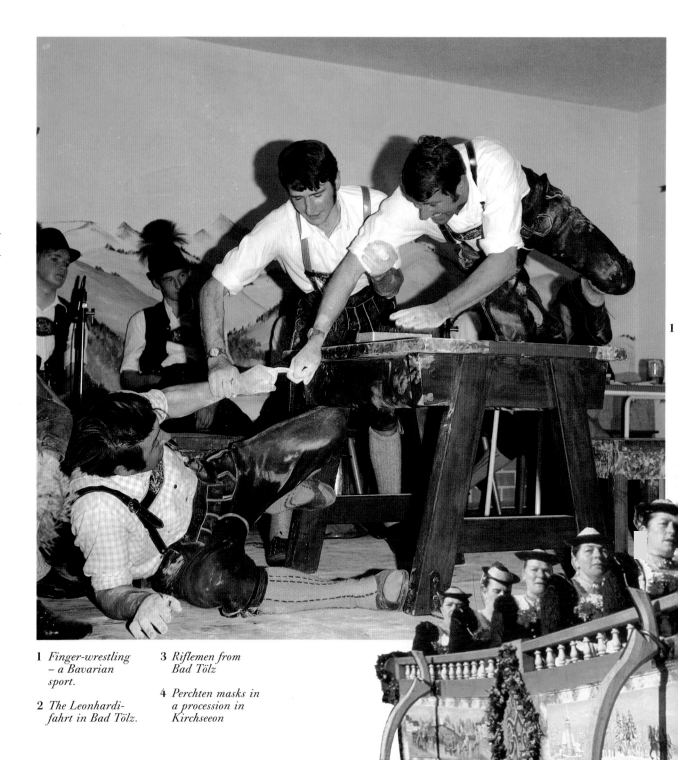

1 *Finger-wrestling – a Bavarian sport.*

2 *The Leonhardi-fahrt in Bad Tölz.*

3 *Riflemen from Bad Tölz*

4 *Perchten masks in a procession in Kirchseeon*

Anyone who considers these traditional customs and practices a barrier to a modern way of life is wrong. On the contrary. Knowledge of one's roots gives people a sense of security. This enables them to face the trends of a new age in an open and objective way without succumbing to its temptations.

Bayern

1 *Clock with
mechanism by
Leopold Hoys
(1750).*

2 *Preserving
momunments
ensures that cer-
tain professions
will always be
required. Restorer
at work.*

1

ince the nineteenth century when the industrial revolution in Germany was well under way, two main forms of craft have existed side by side. The "conservative" artists pursued the type of craft handed down through the ages, others sought other forms of expression unknown up to then. Today, for example, in the Bavarian Forest, there is a centre for glass-blowing and glass production, both local industries: reproducing the old and traditional and striving for something new.

The arts and crafts movement of the nineteenth century was a reaction against the levelling tendencies of mass production. Its aim was to introduce principles of art into the factory. As long ago as 1851 an arts and crafts society was founded in Munich to be followed later by a special school for craft artists.

Around the turn of the century artists were turning away from traditional forms to look for a new language in their craft. Here, too, Bavarian artists had a significant role to play. After the Second World War the experimental jewellery of the Munich Gold Works caused a sensation. Up to the present day ,too, Bavarian potters, glass artists, gold and silversmiths enrich the international art scene with their work.

3 *Building violins – one of the traditional crafts in Bavaria.*

4 *A modern glass painting firm.*

5 *The verre eglomise painter Pankratz Walk.*

1 *The village church in Ober-ammergau.*

Bayern

2

3

4

2 *An example of traditional "Lüftlmalerei". The "Pilatus- haus" in Ober- ammergau.*

3 *Traditional artists' craft in a modern form. Products form the Schmid glass- blowing works in Lionberg, Bavarian Forest.*

4 *A look behind the scenes. Producing glass.*

1 *An attraction for people from all over the world: Munich's Oktoberfest.*

2 *A spectacular event full of pomp and colour: the Kaltenberg Knights.*

3 *A magnificent procession in old costumes: the Fürstenhochzeit in Landshut.*

Bayern

Bavarian gregariousness is well known. All over the world. How otherwise could you explain the number of guests from all parts of the world who come to the Oktoberfest?

The Australians make their annual pilgrimage from the other side of the globe to Munich. The greatest festival in the world attracts millions of visitors to the metropolis on the Isar. The colourful processions with their splendidly decorated horses, the relaxed hustle and bustle on the "Theresienwiese" – for two whole weeks Munich becomes the amusement park of the world. By the way. The one-litre mugs are often filled up with alcohol-free beer nowadays.

But there are other festivals in Bavaria which are also famous all over the World. The "Fürstenhochzeit" in Landshut, for example. Every four years you can see how the Bavarian Duke George led his Polish princess Jadwiga to the altar in 1475.

4 *"The Dragon's Sting" in Furth im Walde.*

5 *Wasservogelsingen (Water Fowl Singing) in Lower Bavaria.*

Every ten years you can experience the unique Passion Play in Oberammergau which has its roots in a vow of 1633 when the village was threatened by the pest during the Thirty Years' War. The whole village is involved in the production which depicts Christ's Passion. The inhabitants

of Oberammergau play the figures from the Bible and in 1990 the Bavarian Prime Minister Max Streibl had a walk-on part as "man in the crowd".

A religious play, which was intended to ban the pest. In 1990, as always, the people from Oberammargau fulfil-led the pledge which their ancestors had made in 1633. Since then no one has in fact died from the pest.

1

2

3

1 The "Wal-
halla" near
Regensburg.

2. Regensburg
Cathedral at
night.

3 When archi-
tects were still
"master buil-
ders". The
town hall in
Augsburg was
built between
1616 and 1620
from the
design of
Andreas Holl.

avaria can even find superlatives to describe its past and present architecture. Take the huge tent-like roof over the Olympic complex in Munich for example. Or Germany's oldest church, the "Marienkapelle" on the "Marienberg" looking over Würzburg which was built in 706. Or the city of Kempten, the oldest in Germany, which also lies within Bavarian's borders.

The importance of architecture for Bavaria, however, cannot just be expressed in figures and dates. Its significance can be attributed to the fact that apart from having a great variety of architecture, Bavaria also saw the Baroque and Rococo periods through to their end.

The Gothic era also left traces in Bavaria. The first great church from this epoch was the Church of St. Lorenz in Nuremberg, the last the "Frauenkirche" in Munich. In the flourishing Fugger city Augsburg the first Renaissance building was erected between 1509 and 1518. The master builder Andreas Holl had a further significant impact on this epoch with his design of Augsburg town hall.

4

53

5

6

4 *An idyll on the Regnitz river. The town hall in Bamberg.*

5 *Dominated by the Middle Ages. The skyline over the old part of Nuremberg.*

6 *The auditorium in the Markgräflich opera house in Bayreuth.*

It was with the Baroque period that Bavarian architecture reached its peak. Bavaria is Baroque. The merriment, fullness of shape, festiveness, variety of colour, vitality and joy of life can be seen in the forms which have been left behind. Munich, Würzburg, Weltenburg, Diessen, Ottobeuren or Fürstenfeldbruck are all testimonies of this epoch.

The Rococo period in Bavaria was no less varied. This art form, dating from the eighteenth century, is best represented in the Munich Residenz, in the Cuvilliés Theatre or the Nymphenburg and Schleißheim castles and, not least, in the Rococo churches which are scattered all over Bavaria.

Under the reign of King Ludwig I (1825-1848) Munich received a new face. The King, interested in science and the arts, found a congenial spirit in his master builder Leo von Klenze, who created buildings, squares and roads whose splendour can still be seen today in the capital city. The Pinakothek, Glypothek, Königsplatz, Hofgarten arcades, the All Saints' Hofkirche. Following Leo von Klenze's traces will take you past

through the historical centre of Munich, into the Ludwigstrasse and beyond.

The destruction of Munich in the Second World War meant that the Fifties and Sixties were decades devoted to building flats and other buildings as quickly as possible. An emphasis on other aspects of architecture came later with, for example, the construction of the Olympic centre and other administrative buildings. This blend of the functional and the artistic has made many of these buildings real eye-catchers in the city.

1 Built for the 1972 Olympics. Even today an attraction for many Munich people and tourists. The Munich Olympic Park.

2 A magnificent building from the seventeenth century: Schleißheim Castle.

3 With its premises in Munich's outskirts Neuperlach, Siemens gave jobs to 10,000 people as well as embarking on a new type of city architecture.

4 One of the most photographed buildings in Munich. The headquarters of the Bavarian Hypotheken und Wechselbank or Hypo.

Bayern

3

The BMW Research and Engineering Centre has been conceived according to new insights in communication science. One advantage: the time needed to develop a car model can be radically reduced. Changes have taken place in the way we live, too. Being in a city but feeling that you are living in a village complete with quieter roads and facilities such as kindergartens, shops and other offices near at hand – this is necessary to attract qualified people to work in Bavaria's firms.

1 *"Kunst am Bau" – the symbol of the GEMA building.*

2/3 *An example of architecture which puts people at the centre. "The Village".*

4 *Contemporary office architecture with a humane touch. The Pallas House in Munich.*

5 *The Munich
Culture Centre,
Gasteig. Seat of
the Philharmonie,
the City Library
and the Adult
Education Centre.*

6 *The Headquarters
of the Sparkasse
or "Savings Bank"
in Munich.*

7 *The City Hilton
Hotel, Munich.*

1 *Lucas Cranach
(1472-1553)
Lamentation
under the Cross
Alte Pinakothek,
Munich.*

2 *Albrecht Dürer
(1471-1528)
The Four Apostles,
John, Peter, Paul,
Mark (1526) Alte
Pinakothek,
Munich.*

"reating forms means living. As man changes, so do his forms".

There is a thread going through the variety of art forms in Bavaria. The works created here often bring together the sum of ideas in an epoch, making one style into a valid form. The work of Albrecht von Altdorfers in the Alte Pinakothek, for example, heralded the ascendancy of the Danube School in the Gothic period. One of his most famous works is the "Alexander Battle".

This thread in Bavarian art stretches from early art forms to documents of the classical Modern Art – the "Blauer Reiter", for example, from whose almanach the introductory quotation has been taken. The pictures and theoretical texts of that famous group of artists who gathered around Wassily Kandinsky and Franz Marc and who at the beginning of the twentieth century put perception and form on a new footing, marked the beginning of the Modern Art in Bavaria. On the other

3

3 *Lovis Corinth (1858–1925) Lake Walchen. The Yellow Meadow (1921). Bavarian State Collection.*

ALEXANDER M.DARIVM VLT: SVPERAT
CÆSIS IN ACIE PERSAR: PEDIT: C. M. EQVIT
VERO X.M. INTERFECTIS. MATRE QVOQVE
CONIVGE.LIBERIS DARII REGIS CVM M.H.AVD
AMPLIVS EQVITIB: FVGA DILAPSI.CAPTIS.

1

hand, the work of these artists who broke with the past also included the Bavarian tradition in art – a splendour of colour, joy and vitality.

Bavaria, but above all Munich, experienced a climax in the arts under the reign of King Ludwig I (reign 1825–1848). As founder and motor of the "periclasean Age" in Bavaria, he was praised and honoured by artists and scientists alike. The legendary King Ludwig II (reign 1864-1886) fled from the everyday world of politics into art and the romanticism. The castles in Neuschwanstein, Linderhof and Herrenchiemsee were built under his direction and are really from a fairy-tale. As a patron of Richard Wagner and the source of finances for the festival theatre in Bayreuth – which today still attracts a high-class mixture of VIPs, aristocracy, leading figures in politics and business – Ludwig II provided Wagner with a framework for his musical dramas which is unique in the world.

Franz von Stucks' "Jugendstil" villa or the ochre-coloured, classicist Lenbachhaus witness the high social standing of painters in Munich at the turn of the century. The Lenbachhaus accommodates one of the most significant collections of Modern Art: the important "Blauer Reiter" pictures in-

cluding those by Marc, Kandinsky, Gabriele Münther and Alexej Jawlensky.

The Schwabing artists scene of the turn of the century still enjoys a legendary reputation today. The fruitful blend of the bohemian, the naive, of "barroom bliss" and

2

1 *Albrecht Altdorfer (ca. 1480-1538) The Battle at Issus 333 BC Alexander Battle (1529) Alte Pinakothek, Munich.*

2 *Wassily Kandinsky (1866-1944) Dreamy Improvisation The State Gallery of Modern Art, Munich.*

3 *Franz Marc (1880–1916) The Panther (1908) Lenbachhaus, Munich.*

3

Bayern

extreme creativity inspired such different characters as Thomas and Heinrich Mann, Stefan George and Franziska von Reventlow. The "biting" magazine Simplicissimus with a bulldog as its trademark, the pub "Alter Simpl" (still a meeting point for artists, celebrities (and other night owls) are characteristic of the period.

The list of important artists who were born in Bavaria or at least completed the majority of their

work here is long. It stretches from Veit Stoß to Albrecht Dürer, to Carl Spitzweg and the painters of the Modern Art mentioned before. Orlando di Lasso, Franz Liszt, Richard Strauß and Carl Orff are also to be found on the list, as is Richard Wagner (although he was born in Saxony).

1 *Mozart's "Magic Flute", directed by August Everding, at the Munich Opera. With Wolfgang Brendel as Papageno.*

2 *Carl Spitzweg (1808-1885) The Poor Poet (1839) Neue Pinakothek, Munich.*

3 *Bavaria's most famous twentieth century literary son, Bertolt Brecht in Augsburg. The original photograph is in the Munich City Museum.*

In literature Bavaria played a prominent role early on. The oldest documents containing German writing, the "Wessobrunner Gebet", were found in Upper Bavaria. Two of the leading writers from the Middle Ages, Wolfram von Eschenbach and Walther von der Vogelweide, were "children of Bavaria" as were – in the true sense of the words – the authors Ludwig Ganghofer and Ludwig Thoma. Bertolt Brecht, Bavaria's best known twentieth century literary son, came from Augsburg. Another, the Nobel Prize winner Thomas Mann, was born in Lübeck but wrote much of his work in Munich.

5

63

4

6

4 *Modern museum architecture: the Neue Pinakothek in Munich.*

5 *Wagner's "Rheingold". Nikolaus Lehnhoff's production in Munich. The scenery by Erich Wonder caused an international sensation.*

6 *Franz von Lenbach (1836-1904) Richard Wagner (around 1874/5), Lenbachhaus, Munich.*

Bayern

Beautiful landscape and countless cultural attractions bring about 20 million tourists to Bavaria annually: walkers, skiers and surfers as much as friends of the arts, connoisseurs of architecture or those on a cure.

From the pulsating art centre Munich to the rugged nature of the Bavarian Forest. From the chalk rocks of the Bavarian Alps to the undulating hills of the Low Mountain Range or the lakes around cities like Würzburg, Bamberg or Passau. Bavaria offers variety!

Needless to say, tourism is an aspect of the economy that should not be underestimated – particularly for the more rural regions like the Bavarian Forest where many of the jobs are to be found in the tourist industry.

There are about 300,000 people in Bavaria who live on tourism. According to the number of beds available and hotel reservations made, Bavaria ranks top in the hotel league. The environment in Bavaria, still relatively intact, is clearly an important economic fact and not to be underrated.

In order to strengthen Bavaria's position as number 1 tourist state and to protect its "capital", the clean environment, a number of measures have been taken under the motto "Quieter Tourism". Reducing the noise from traffic, saving energy, avoiding the production of rubbish, waste management, caring for the countryside. Those keen on protecting the enviroment are particularly concerned about the Alps, which, having been opened up totally to tourists, are now in danger of being "run over".

1

2

3

1 *One of the most splendid of King Ludwig II's buildings is Linderhof Castle.*

2 *The Kurhaus or "Cure House" in Bad Tölz.*

3 *Art attracts people like a magnet. The Alte Pinakothek in Munich.*

4 *A scene near Bad Wiessee in Upper Bavaria.*

5 *Munich's famous beergarden. The Chinese Tower in the English Garden.*

6 *The promenade in Wiessee.*

Bayern

The so-called "Romantic Road" goes from north to south through the white and blue Free State. The cultural and scenic treasures in Bavaria are stretched out along it like a pearl necklace. The river Main and the hills covered with grapes dominate the landscape around Würzburg. The route goes through the Tauber Valley, past famous Rothenburg and on to the areas Ries, Lechfeld and Pfaffenwinkel to the castles at the foot of the Alps.

The Residenz in Würzburg is one of the most distinguished buildings of Balthasar Neumann and is just as much worth a visit as Veitshöchheim nearby. In the Tauber Valley you can discover the pictures of the Franconian wood-carver Tilman Riemenschneider. A climax along the way: the newly restored Wies Church, which is considered one of the most famous Rococo buildings in the world. The castles Hohenschwangau and Neuschwanstein are a suitable end to a route which is justified in being called the Romantic Road.

With its combination of scenic charm, culturally historic treasures and Franconian and Swabian

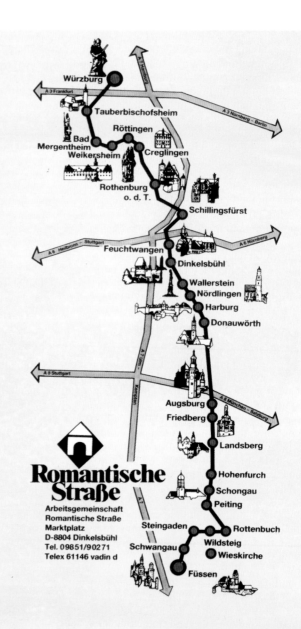

hospitality, the Romantic Road offers the tourist an attractive insight into the many facets of Bavarian life.

1 *The Residenz in Würzburg.*

2 *Rothenburg ob der Tauber.*

3 *An old half-timbered house.*

4 *Like pearls on a string. The most romantic corner of Germany.*

3

The Constitution and Parliament

"Bavaria is a Free State" it says in the first paragraph of the first article in the Bavarian constitution. This means the monarchy has been abolished and it is now a republic. A modern democratic state with a freely elected government. The border signs with the words "Free State of Bavaria" leave no doubt in the minds of travellers in Germany. Bavaria is different.

Of course it is fully integrated into the German federation, yet it still retains its individual character and identity, developed and consolidated through a 1,000-year old history.

The words "Free State" are also an indication of Bavaria's political position within Germany. Rejecting every form of overpowering centralism, Bavaria sees itself as the vanguard of federalism.

Safeguarding its interests means at the same time serving a political culture which supports federalism, accepts differences and allows opposition.

The Coat of Arms

On 5 June, 1950 the Bavarian Coat of Arms was established by law. Its symbols have their origins in Bavarian history.

Golden Lion

For centuries the golden lion on a black background served as a sign for the old-Bavarian and Palatinate Wittelsbachs. Today it is linked to the administrative district of the Upper Palatinate.

Franconian Rake

Three prongs showing upwards divide the white and red square. In around 1350 this "rake" established itself as the coat of arms in the diocese of Würzburg. From 1410 on the prince-bishops used it as their seal. Today it symbolizes Upper, Central and Lower Franconia.

Blue Panther

The Lower Bavarian Pfalzgrafen von Ortenburg first used the blue panther on a white square before it was taken over by the Wittelsbachs. Today it represents Lower and Upper Bavaria.

Three Black Lions

The three black lions on a golden background which stare at you when you look at them have been taken from the old coat of arms of

the Hohenstaufen. Today they belong to the administrative district of Swabia.

Blue and white heart-shaped shield

The heart-shaped shield with white (silver) and blue diamonds was taken from Graf von Bogen by the Wittelsbachs in 1247. Today it is "the" symbol for Bavaria. Inofficially it is referred to as the "Small Coat of Arms".

The People's Crown

The crown on the top of the coat of arms consists of a golden circle decorated with jewels and five ornamental leaves. The crown symbolizes the rule and sovereignty of the people following the end of the monarchy.

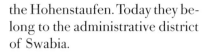

Bavaria is not only the largest and oldest German state, it is also one of the oldest states in Europe.

Bavarian history began when the Roman Empire was disintegrating. In 500 AD the Teutons brought the rule of the Romans to an end. Those Romans who had remained together with the Teutons joined the original Celtic inhabitants – according to the most recent research – to make a Bavarian tribe. As long ago as the sixth century a centre of power established itself in Bavaria. Under the Agilofinger and later in the tenth century under the supremacy of the Guelphs, a powerful dukedom was formed, whose authority was nearly that of its own monarch.

At the same time as these developments were taking place Christianity reached the Bavarian area. Henry the Lion (1156-1180) was an outstanding regent in Bavaria's history and it was he who founded Munich in 1158. The Emperaor Barbarossa deposed Henry in 1180 and passed over his power and authority to the Wittelsbachs, who in the following centuries had a decisive role to

War hardly weakened Bavaria's position. On the contrary. The Upper Palatinate became part of it. During the periods of Baroque and Rococo it underwent a phase of cultural productivity and creativity. The splendour, beauty and wealth of forms which resulted from this age overwhelm the observer even today.

At the turn of the nineteenth century Bavaria was faced with a difficult constellation of power. Max IV placed his country under Napoleon's protection.

On January 1, 1806 Max IV became King Max I and declared Bavaria a member of the Confederation of the Rhine.

play in the country's history. In striving for power Bavaria extended its territories immensely. Ludwig the Bavarian (1302-1347) took over Holland, Tyrol,

Hennegau and Mark Brandenburg. Following this need for expansion the House of Wittelsbach experienced a weakening of its influence in the fourteenth and fifteenth centuries.

Although it developed a foothold in many areas of Franconia and Swabia, the Reformation had less success in Old-Bavaria, where a bastion of the counter-reformation established itself in the second half of the sixteenth century.

The horror of the Thirty Years'

1 *A complete picture of a city. Nördlingen im Ries.*

2 *Max I Monument in front of Munich's National Theatre.*

3 *The Bavaria looking over the Theresienwiese in Munich.*

4 *The oldest housing scheme in the world: the Fuggerei in Augsburg.*

During the war of liberation Bavaria joined sides with Napoleon's adversaries. An important step on the way to political democracy was the constitution of 1808. There, for the first time, equality of all Bavarians before the law, the security of all individuals and their property, the independence of the justice and freedom of conscience were laid down. This led to the first Bavarian constitution of 1818. From this year on, the new parliament, consisting of federal councillors chambers and the members of parliament, took

an active part in the formation of policies for governing Bavaria.

In 1833 Bavaria joined the German Customs Union. Under Ludwig I Munich began to flourish as Germany's cultural centre: the arts and sciences also blossomed. With the promotion of trade and commerce Ludwig I created the economic basis for a "new Renaissance". The first German railway, from Nuremberg to Fürth, which was opened in 1835, demonstrated the prosperity of the epoch. Following the revolution of March 1848 Ludwig I abdicated and passed his official duties

1 *Built according to the Wagnerian model. The Venus grotto of King Ludwig II.*

2 *The Mirror Room in Herrenchiemsee.*

3 *The splendid staircase in Herrenchiemsee Castle.*

4 *Neuschwanstein Castle.*

5 *Supporter of the arts, builder of the Neuschwanstein, Herrenchiemsee and Linderhof castles: King Ludwig II.*

4

over to his son, Maximilian II. He, too, encouraged the arts and sciences immensely and was very much in favour of socio-political reforms as well.

During the reign of Ludwig II (1864-1886), who even today is known as the "fairy-tale King", Bavaria was involved in the Prussian and the Franco-German Wars. In 1871 Bavaria joined the German Empire. It was less his military achievements which explain Ludwig II's continuing popularity but rather his retreat from politics into a fairy-tale world of castles and romantic visions of Wagner's music. Even today Neuschwanstein Castle is one of the most famous and frequently visited buildings in the world. The life of Ludwig II and

5

his mysterious death in Lake Starnberg in 1886 have been the subject of many a legend, book and film ever since. Ludwig's uncle, the Prince Regent Luitpold (1886- 1912) and his son Ludwig III (1912-1918) mark the end of the Wittelsbachs, a House which had determined Bavaria's fortunes for 738 years.

In the confusion following the First World War a councillors republic ruled for a short time in Bavaria, until, on 12 August 1919, the parliament established a constitution on the basis of a parliamentary democracy.

Hitler's putsch in 1923 came at a time of exploding inflation. In the same year the Reichsmark was introduced as the currency in Bavaria. During the Nazi dictatorship from 1933-45 Bavaria lost all its sovereign authority.

On 1 December 1946 the people of Bavaria voted in a referendum for a new constitution. With the passing of the Basic Law in Germany Bavaria became a "Land" within the Federal Republic of Germany. Even after German reunification on 3 October 1990 Bavaria remained Germany's largest state.

Bayern

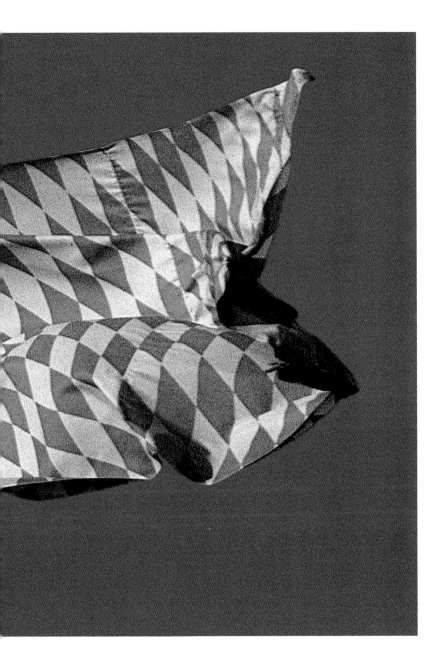

Bavarian history in short

179 AD Regensburg is made a
Roman colony

6th century Formation of
Bavarian Dukedom

738-42 St. Bonifatius and Duke
Odilo establish Bavarian
church organisation

1158 Henry the Lion founds
Munich

1180 Otto von Wittelsbach recei-
ves the Dukedom of Bavaria
from Emperor Barbarossa

15/16th century Trade and commerce booms

1662-1726 Prince Max Emanuel
encourages Barock influen-
ces in Bavaria

1806 Bavaria becomes a kingdom
under Max I Joseph

1818 New constitution

1825-48 King Ludwig I Munich
becomes a glittering capital
and a centre for sciences

1848-64 Support for arts and
sciences under Maximilian II

1864-86 Bavaria, under Ludwig II,
takes part in wars against
Prussia and France

1919 Councillors Republic, new
constitution

1933 End of sovereignty under
Hitler's dictatorship

1946 Third Bavarian constitution

1949 Establishment of the Federal
Republic of Germany

1990 German reunification

s the crowning end of the Maximilianstrasse, Munich's most sought-after address for international companies, boutiques and jewellers, the Maximilianeum, Bavaria's parliament, towers over the Isar river. Looking out from the archways of this splendid building, the view can roam over the city.

The foundation stone was laid on 6 October 1857 under the reign of Maximilian II. Apart from marking the architectural completion of the Maximilianstrasse, the building was also to accommodate a foundation for extremely gifted school-leavers. The King, known for his wide range of interests, was intending to develop an elite school where future civil servants could be assisted.

The foundation still exists today. And as in the past the students, whose old boys include the physicist Werner Heisenberg and the ex prime minister Franz Josef Strauss, live in the Maximilianeum.

Since January 1949 members of

1 *The Maximilianneum – seat of the Bavarian parliament and the Senate.*

2 *The seat of local administration: Augsburg town hall.*

the Bavarian parliament have shared the Maximilianeum with the students. In the years before, however, due to the bombing during the Second World War, a number of provisional premises had to be found for the politicians.

Parliamentarism has a long tradition in Bavaria. The first constitution in Germany came into being in 1818 in Bavaria. With the councillors republic of 1919 the monarchy disappeared completely and a par-

3 _The eleventh Bavarian parliament in 1990._

4 _The prime minister's oath._

liamentary democracy was introduced in its place. After a referendum the third (and last) Bavarian constitution became law on 1 December 1946. Every four years the members of the Bavarian parliament are elected in free, equal and direct elections. The highest authority in the land is the state government which is elected by the members of the parliament. It comprises the prime minister, the ministers and the under-secretaries. During its period in power the government determines main policies. Passing laws requires the consent of parliament.

A speciali feature of the Bavarian constitution is the Senate whose members are appointed from industrial, cultural, social or communal bodies. Functioning as a kind of modern professional representative organisation it has above all an advisory role to play although it can submit bills to parliament, too.

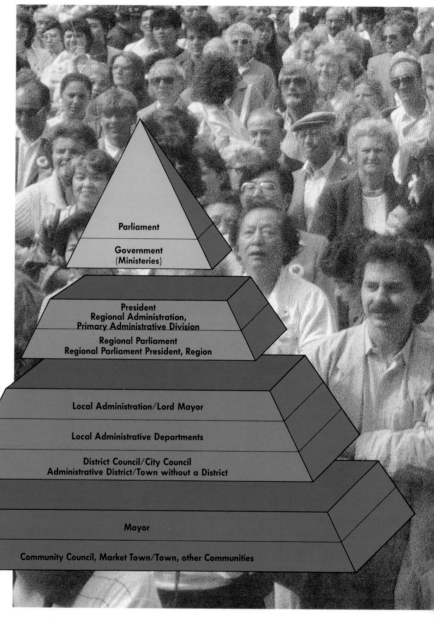

The institutions of Bavarian politics are elected by the people in free elections.

The middle level of the state administrative system is made up of the seven regional districts Upper Bavaria, Lower Bavaria, Swabia, Upper Palatinate, Upper Franconia, Central Franconia and Lower Franconia with their regional parliaments. The local administrative departments in the 71 administrative districts including the towns which do not belong to a district comprise the lower level of the system. The community bodies carry out important administrative tasks in local coucils. They include seven local administrations, 71 administrative districts and 2,026 communities.

83

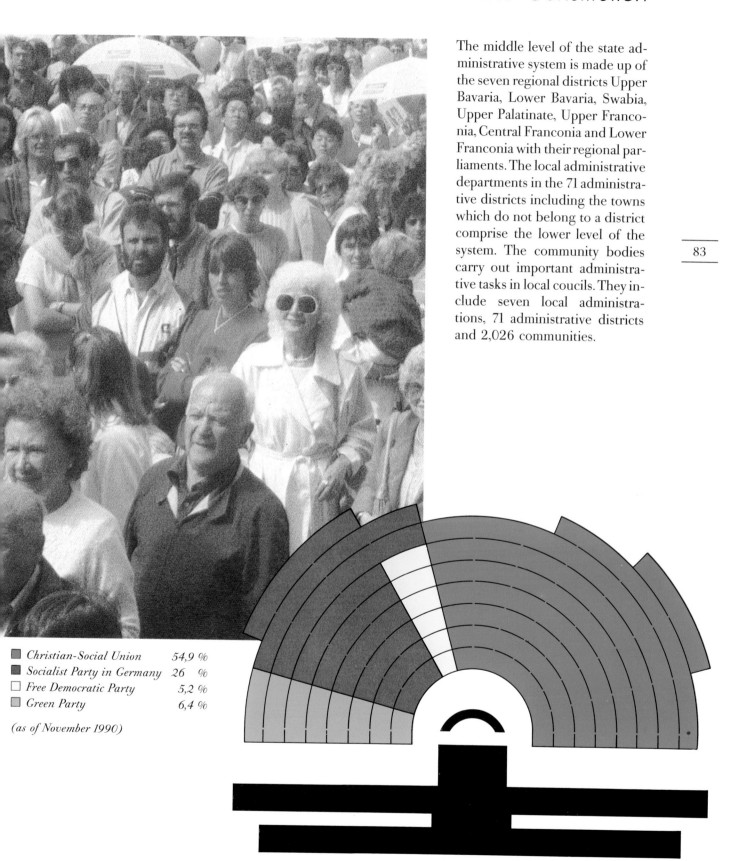

	Christian-Social Union	*54,9 %*
	Socialist Party in Germany	*26 %*
	Free Democratic Party	*5,2 %*
	Green Party	*6,4 %*

(as of November 1990)

When in 1949 the Federal Republic of Germany was established, its political principles being proclaimed in the Basic Law, Bavaria joined this Federation as a state which could look back over a 1,000-year old history. And although in subsequent decades it saw itself pledged to the democratic values of a state under the rule of law, it still insisted on the preservation of its own identity and the support of federalistic principles as the cornerstone of a free order.

In the Bavarian State Ministry for European and German State Affairs, Bavarian activites are coordinated. The Bavarian representation in Bonn is just as active in promoting its political objectives as it is in portraying its interests to the public.

Once again. Bavaria is not only one of the oldest states in Europe, it also has a great deal of weight in economic terms. With a gross domestic product (GDP) of over 400 billion DM it beats half the EEC member states. The growth rates, too, are well above the EEC average. The Bavarian economy is very much export oriented with almost 50% of its exports going to other EEC countries. In 1989 Bavaria recorded a record surplus of 21.5 billion DM. Only in the area of raw products do the imports exceed the exports.

However impressive these figures may be, they do not say much about the structural strength of the Bavarian economy. The positive effect of political stability, social peace, a predictable, long-term economic policy and a first-class vocational training system can best be measured in terms of productivity, the manufacturing intensity and quality of the employees per unit of time. Along with the Swiss, Bavaria is top of the league here, too. Other indications of a healthy economy are the high number of people in employment (61%) and the lowest rate of unemployment in the EEC. On the one hand high wages and salaries might be considered a disadvantage, but on the other hand it may be proof of high qualifications and standards amongst the employees.

The Bavarian economy does not mind spending on its excellent human resources.

As in the rest of Germany so in the EEC Bavaria sees itself as the vanguard of federalism and the enemy of a concentration of power in the centre. An important

*Bavarian House
in Brussels*

step in this direction was taken under the direction of the Bavarian prime minister when in 1989 the "Europe of Regions" conference convened.

In Europe Bavaria has had an office in Brussels since 1987 and been available as a partner to talk to ever since. The office is a communication centre and point of contact between the State of Bavaria and any European bodies, bringing citizens, businesses and organisations to the discussion table.

These measures are backed up with meetings of European experts from the different ministeries. The special offices dealing with European affairs keep a close eye on the interests of Europe when making political and other decisions.

With its fortunate blend of the traditional and the modern, of global thinking and local commitments, Bavaria can claim to be a model for a future united Europe. It has maintained on the one side a distinctive identity, show-

ing its own profile and character and always being ready for a constructive argument.

On the other hand it is more than any other German state open for the future. Bavaria is one of the most technically innovative and economically dynamic states, integrated into the cultural, political and economic developments in Europe and the rest of the world. Its heart is in Bavaria but its mind thinks in global dimensions.

85

4

Craftsmen's Trades

1 *Traditional Maypole in Münsing.*

2 *At the time they were called glass-makers: the first picture of an optician in Nuremberg from the year 1568.*

Bayern

raftsmen's trades have accompanied and helped to shape Bavaria's history over the last 1,000 years. The most influential representatives of the trades in the Middle Ages were the guilds, powerful organisations with a say in matters, not least in the way life was run in the towns and cities. From their establishment in the eleventh and twelfth centuries up to 1868 when in Bavaria freedom of trade was introduced, craftsmen's trades were organised by the guilds, which meant that only members of a guild could work in a trade. The function of the guilds went far beyond representing their members' interests as we might understand it today. They were in fact responsible for questions of training and promotion, determining the requirements for the masters examination and regulating the prices for their goods and services with the authorities. As professional organisations of partly religious character and with social welfare functions, the guilds cultivated customs which lent colour to cultural life and which in many fields have remained alive today. A popular occasion for ceremony and jokes of every description was the "Gesellen-Machen" – the recognition of apprentices as qualified craftsmen and as such, fully recognised guild members. In a rather boisterous ritual the transition from apprentice to honourable qualified craftsman was celebrated with the poor candidates usually landing in a spring up to their necks in water.

Today the dances of the different trades are still famous – the well-known Schäffler Dance, for example, or the dance of the coopers, where the Munich, Augsburg or Nuremberg versions were staged with particular lavish and colour.

2

1 *Stonemason in traditional clothes.*

2 *Schäffler in the Oktoberfest procession.*

The tried and tested method is called the "dual training system". This is the way German trainees are prepared in courses lasting usually three years for their future professions.

The German trainee system is considered exemplary by other nations. More and more states from all over the world are expressing interest in the German practice. The principle of giving practical training in the company or workshop and supplementing it with theory in a vocational school has proved to be an ideal way of doing things. At the same time other subjects are taught so that the trainee also develops interests in other fields apart from his own narrow subject. The comprehensive, thorough training in

a trade that these young specialists receive is one of the reasons why the phrase "Made in Germany" is held in such high regard all over the world. In the future, too, even higher demands will be asked of these qualified craftsmen to ensure that they retain their leading position within the European market.

Bavaria has recognised this fact and has decided on a whole bundle of measures. Courses in other companies, for example, are now available to trainees whose training firms have specialized in one field or who do have all the facilities their better-equipped colleagues do. There are also measures which specifically support young women, particularly in typical men's professions as well as training programmes for

With its combination of inhouse training and courses in a vocational school the German trades have set new international standards .

young foreigners which takes issue with the sort of problems they may later face and for pupils from special schools or those with learning problems. The extension of the year between school and the start of a training course can be included here, too.

In order to guarantee that young people to make the right decision for a long-term career, many firms now offer school-leavers the chance to start an appenticeship in a certain job for the purpose of finding out whether it corresponds to their skills and inclinations.

With the examination at the end of the course, the trainee demonstrates that he is able to work independently in his profession. Again, when compared with international competition, Bavaria comes out very well. At the "trial of strength" for international trades from all over the world which takes place at the "Profession Olympics", the representatives

from Bavaria regularly come in first position.

The jewel of the training system for cratsmen's trades is the title "master". Every year in Bavaria about 9,000 qualified craftsmen take the exam to become a master – and more than 10 per cent of these are women, with the number increasing. The opportunities for a new master are superb: either a leading position in one of the countless firms or starting a business of your own. The state supports the setting up of new companies by offering credit at a lower rate of interest.

A lot of practice and as much theory as they need – with this the trainees can face the future with confidence.

Small or middle-sized companies make up a respectable part of the German economy. A strong pillar of the Mittelstand economy are the trades. With approximately 950,000 employees the 135,500 Bavarian firms working in the trades record a turnover of 135 billion DM per year, or about 12% of the total GDP in Bavaria. That means in terms of the overall economy the trades are the second most powerful sector behind industry, but clearly in front of trade and agriculture.

The versatility, qualification and love of innovation of the Bavarian trades makes a decisive contribution to the dynamism and competitiveness of the Bavarian economy. Goldsmith, bookbinder, baker, butcher, fountain constructor, umbrella builder, one-man business or a company with hundreds of staff – they all produce goods and offer services which we could not do without.

The wide spectrum of 125 recognised professions is testimony to the individuality and complexity of the craftsmen's trades. It ranges from optician to string-instrument maker, from wine cellarman to hearing aid acoustician, from lithographer to box maker, from the modern such as office information electronic engineer to the traditional like violin constructor, which by the way is now extremely popular among young people again.

The 125 trade professions are divided into seven groups:
- Building and extending trade
- Metal trade

1 *Not all products can be made by machines. Particularly large insulators and other special constructions* *are produced – as here at Siemens in Redwitz – in a so-called garnishing process. Experience and manual skills play a decisive role.*

- Wood trade
- Clothing, textile and leather trade
- Food trade
- Health and personal hygiene trade as well chemical and cleaning trade
- Glass, paper, ceramics and other trades

With an investment total of more than five billion DM a year for tools, machines, equipment and premises, the trades increase their competitiveness and certainly boost the economy. With flexibility, love of innovation and high performance, these firms belong to the most advanced in Germany.

Such commitment bears fruit: the order books in most firms are well filled. Anyone who knows how to launch tailor-made products and services on to the market with the necessary marketing know-how has excellent prospects. Suppliers specialised in a certain field or repair and maintenance firms have the best perspectives. But also small companies can do well by being flexible, reacting to customers' needs

and finding a niche for themselves.

The success of the trades could never have come about without the consistent support of Bavarian economic policy. From the very beginning Bavaria has considered the craftsmen's trades as the cornerstone of the Mittelstand and as such worthy of particular attention. Today craftsmen's companies have many ways of making use of the low-interest loans on offer. In support of training and further training programmes outside the individual com-

panies a dense network of training and technology centres were erected. The levels of training attained by the German trades enjoys the highest reputation throughout the world. Highly

qualified staff are a company's most valuable asset. Craftsmen have long turned this knowledge into action.

The seven regional trade chambers and the unions provide firms with a great deal of support. Those who are self-employed or those who would like to be so, for example, can get a wealth of advice on such questions as investing, planning finances, accounting, choosing a site, company organisation, marketing or the possibilities of exporting. The chances of becoming "business administrator for craftsmen's trades" is a splendid opportunity for those wanting to acquire the knowledge and skills to lead a firm.

EDP advisors are also at the dis-

posal of trade firms, giving individual help and suggestions on how to incorporate computer systems into the everyday running of a business.

With the rate at which technology is progressing small and medium-sized firms can scarcely keep pace with the development in new machines, materials and techniques.

Here, too, the trade organisations have experienced advisors available whose function as mediators at the interface between science and research on the one hand and practical experience in the trades on the other hand is indispensable. Technology transfer is the solution for bringing those

insights from science to the firms which require them.

The Bavarian Ministry for Economics and Transport encourages

– the development of an efficient infrastructure for the transfer of research and technology

– innovative development plans in small and medium-sized firms, and

– within the framework of a technology advisory service for the Mittelstand, the setting up of a specialist advisory panel of external experts

The following organisations also offer advice and support to trade firms:

- the technological advisory service of the craftsmen's trades at the trades chambers
- the transfer offices of the state trade institution
- the transfer offices at the polytechnics, universities and chambers of trade and commerce
- the east and west Bavarian technology transfer institute, OTTI and WETTI

New initiatives like the Charlottenhof Technology and Innovation Centre near Schwandorf

Examples for handicraft art: door knockers in Reichenbach Monastery and a stand at the "Auer Dult" in Munich.

are not only of a model character in Bavaria. These measures have made significant contributions to the retention of a healthy, multi-faceted economic structure shaped by the Mittelstand and made up of a host of partners of different size all complementing each other. Countless companies are working as suppliers to the industry – the best example for this is the car manufacturing industry. It has shown how trade firms with their first-class achievements have given Bavarian industry its worldwide reputation.

*From carpenter to
chimney sweep –
aspects of the
Bavarian trades.*

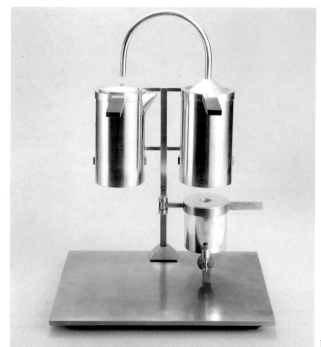

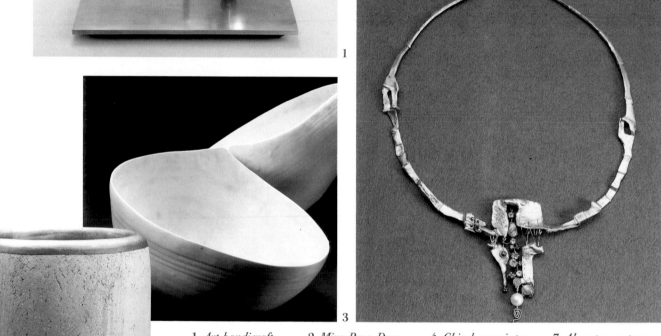

1 *Art handicraft and modern design has always found favour with the public: An espresso machine by Paul Müller. Awarded a special prize by the Danner Foundation in 1987.*

2 *Mira Prus, Danner prize winner, created this double-walled bowl.*

3 *Karen Müller was awarded the Danner Prize in 1987 for this pair of bowls.*

4 *Chip-box painter.*

5 *Neck jewellery by Hermann Jünger, Danner Collection.*

6 *Arts and crafts past and present A brooch with rubins, olives and opals and made from gold and silver by Karl Rothmüller, 1898.*

7 *Almost a century later the artist Vera Rhodius created a series of brooches in gold and silver. Danner Collection.*

8 *Example of the splendid art from previous centuries. Detail from the high altar in Osterhofen.*

Bayern

uality is in. Anyone who can afford it likes to have goods and articles made individually by hand and not mass produced. Traditional arts and crafts benefit from this trend.

In the workshops of gold and silversmiths, weavers, basket makers, sculptors, woodcarvers, glass formers – just to mention a few – works of art are created which in their variety and creativity cannot be seen everywhere.

In Bavaria the promotion of arts and crafts has a long tradition.

In the nineteenth century, during the reign of Ludwig II, it experienced a period of great prosperity. Ludwig placed orders in great quantities giving above all the goldsmithing industry a new impulse. Even today the support from the state makes a valuable contribution to high standards of art handicraft in Bavaria.

Not only state institutions play a role in supporting these small firms. Private organisations are extremely active, too.
Since 1920 the Benno and Therese Danner'sche Art and Craft In-

dustry Foundation has been involved in encouraging Bavarian handicraft and the training prospects of young artists. In 1984 the Foundation announced a competition which every three years awarded prizes to first class achievements in art and craft work thereby hoping to gain more publicity for the industry.

103

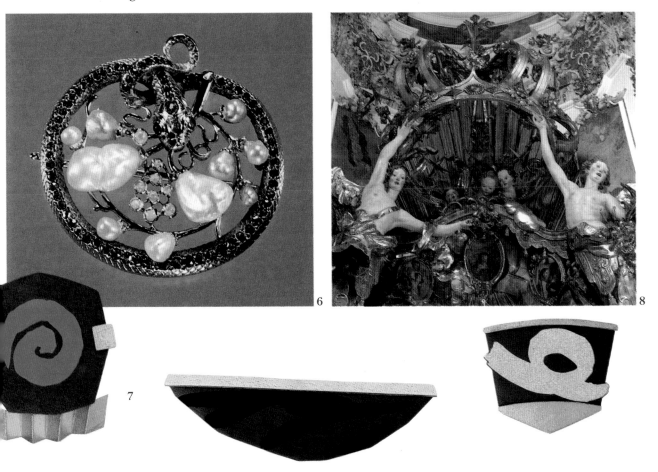

6

7

8

How would a symphony, an opera or chamber music sound without expertly produced instruments. Building musical instruments is an art, which quite literally serves the arts. Oboe, clarinet, saxophone, flute, violin, guitar, zither or organ: all these instruments are made in Bavarian firms specialized in this craft.

People have more leisure time than they did ten or fifteen years ago. Anyone wanting to spend his life doing meaningful and creative things will turn increasingly to music, particularly folk music, the result being an impetus for the Bavarian art and craft industry.

Throughout Bavaria the industry records a turnover of a quarter of a billion DM annually. In the border regions, where most of the work is carried out, there are, for example, 22 firms which

build pianos and harpsichords, 18 which build brass instruments and drums, 16 which build string instruments, 23 which build violins and another 29 which build organs and harmoniums.

In international competitions where standards of musical instruments are compared, Bavarian firms rely on quality. Their instruments are made to meet the highest requirements.

Discussing the needs of the musicians is part of the production process nowadays. Only this way can the firms perfect the quality of their instruments and satisfy the real needs of their clients.

Another sign which demonstrates that the future of the industry has good perspectives is the demand in the firms for positions such as an apprentice. For young people with intuition, manual skills and music in their ears being a musical instrument builder is a dream job.

1 *Rotating organ signed "Xaver Bruder Waldkirch im Max 1869". With ten moving figures.*

2 *Figure clock "Bärentreiber". Augsburg around 1580/9.*

3 *The Bavarian musical instrument building industry is dominated by the regions, above all by Lower Bavaria and the Upper Palatinate*

4 *A violin builder in his workshop.*

The art and craft industry in Bavaria is based in the regions where the business has a history and tradition of its own.

The Bavarian Forest, for example, is a centre for glass production. The most important town is Zwiesel, where you can find the state vocational training centre for glasswork, the oldest training institution of its kind in Germany and the second oldest in the world. The second best-known site is in the Upper Palatine Forest.

The Bavarian glass firms work

most of all with crystal glass and lead crystal. The high export figures for their blown and hand-cut glass is a testimony to the quality and popularity of their products.

Apart from the large glass works there are countless firms with only two or three staff which also contribute to the productive climate in the region. Numerous internationally renowned glass artists based in the Bavarian Forest are a lasting influence on the use of forms in this field of art.

1 *Young people are particularly fond of the art of pottery.*

2 *Blowing glass combines an artistic touch and handicraft perfection.*

3 *Glass products from the Bavarian Forest enjoy an excellent reputation all over the world. Here art from the glass works Schmid in Lindberg.*

4 *Dominikus Auliczek created this porcelain figure of the god of war Mars around 1770.*

106

Bayern

4

5

From Agriculture
to Industry

he change from an agricultural country bottom of the league in the German economy to a European high-tech centre and powerful economic partner for foreign businessmen and investors came as a surprise to some people. It happened so unspectacularly and yet so full of determination that some can no longer discern the "two Bavarias". Here high-tech, dynamism and growth, there traditional costumes, folk music and the shaving brush on the hat.

When, in 1945, people rolled up their sleeves to clear away the ruins that had been left after the Second World War and to build up an economic foundation enabling them to start a new life in freedom and democracy, the

situation in Bavaria looked anything else but good. A country dominated by agriculture and absent of a forward-looking economy, an unattractive position in the corner of the Federal Republic, far away from the coal deposits of the Ruhr, wedged in between the Iron Curtain and the Alps – this was Bavaria.

What happened then proved that there was no basis whatsoever for

this pessimism. People's expectations paled in the face of the real developments. The essential factors contributing to the recovery were:

– far-sighted economic and structural policies

– the setting up of an efficient infrastructure, above all roads

– providing tax and credit incentives for free enterprise

1 *A lesson in a school showing signs of the war.*

2/3 *A scene of devastation like this was common throughout Bavaria, not only in Munich.*

Bayern

2

3

4

– consistent support for small and middle-sized firms

– help for those innovative industries and services with high productivity but low raw material requirements which are looking for a site for their premises

– provision of energy requirements at reasonable prices

– concepts for regional and state planning which are oriented to the future

– site advantages with a clean environment, high recreation value and a Bavarian way of life

4 *A stable, reliable provision of cheap energy is a prerequisite for economic growth.*

Bayernwerk AG is an enterprise operating throughout Bavaria to provide electricity to most regions.

is the home of German space and aeronautics technology, the computer industry, a stronghold of the car manufacturing industry with Audi and BMW and the seat of countless important companies in the machine and automation construction industry. In the list of leading electronic centres in the world, Munich and its surroundings ranks fourth after Silicon Valley, the Boston area and Kyushu in Japan.

Innovation and creativity have been prospering here for a long time. Take the diesel engine or the first German railway or the first pocket watch as examples – they all saw the light of day under the Bavarian sky.

As many as ten Nobel prize winners lived and completed their research after the Second World War in Bavaria, including Werner Heissenberg and Konrad Lorenz.

The three cities of Nuremberg, Fürth and Erlangen as well as the region of Munich made a name for themselves after the war as focus points for new industries.

Those companies which set up shops there did not depend too much on raw materials. Of crucial importance for those firms was, and is, a regular supply of energy, conditions which encouraged the interests of companies, good travel connections, a stable social climate and the availability of qualified workers. Increasingly more attention is being paid to leisure time and recreation facilities open to people in work. Bavaria can offer both.

The road was now clear for Bavaria's rapid rise to becoming a high-tech centre. Today Bavaria

1 A cornerstone of Bavarian energy supply is nuclear power.

2 Even in Bavarian's oldest coal-fired power station in Schwandorf, which went into operation in 1930, something i being done for the environment. This fume cleaner on the fume desulphurizing apparatus is of impressive dimensions, with a height of 50 metres and a diameter of 18 metres

Bayern

Bavaria's journey from agricultural country to high-tech state took place in five clear steps.

1945-1955

After the war the most urgent task was to rebuild what had been destroyed. Old firms were reopened new jobs were created. Furthermore, the 2 million people who had been driven out of their homes between 1933 and 1945 had to be integrated into economic life.

1955-1966

Productivity in the existing firms was intensified, new companies were

3

founded. The result was industrial progress second to none.

1966-1973

The first recession in the Federal Republic hit the economy hard revealing Bavaria's economic weaknesses. The government reacted with improvements in

structural policy leading to a boom in subsequent years.

4

3 *A process with a future. At the beginning of 1990 almost 6,000 solar modules in the solar-hydrogen plant in Neunburg v. Wald provided electricity to the national grid for the first time.*

4/5 *Good air connections are an important aspect of an efficient infrastructure.*

5

1974-1982

A worldwide explosion the price of oil caused another recession. In 1978 the situation improved but a second rise in the early eighties dampened progress. The only state to survive the crisis without harming its overall economic performance was Bavaria.

Since 1982

Bavaria remained the frontrunner among the German states in terms of economic growth. Above-average performance in all areas prove this.

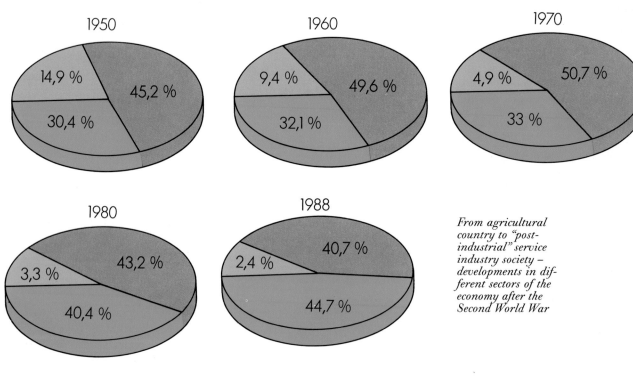

1950

14,9 %
45,2 %
30,4 %

1960

9,4 %
49,6 %
32,1 %

1970

4,9 %
50,7 %
33 %

1980

3,3 %
43,2 %
40,4 %

1988

2,4 %
40,7 %
44,7 %

From agricultural country to "post-industrial" service industry society – developments in different sectors of the economy after the Second World War

◻ *Agriculture and Forestry*
◻ *Production*
◻ *Services/Trade/Transport*

"Bavaria – a progressive and competitive economic partner. Bavaria's economy is open, dominated by small and middle-sized firms and oriented to the future. It is considered one of the most dynamic in Europe. Flexibility, quality and modern technolgy pay off here – and for the environment, too.

Bavarian economic policy is built on fair competition. At the same time it aims to provide an economic climate which fosters excellent results as well as investment and innovation. This way it creates high employment and a good standard of living, too. Policies for the regions, for technology and for small and medium-sized firms have their role to play as much as policies for energy, transport and telecommunications."

August R. Lang
Bavarian Minister of Economics
and Transport

griculture dominates the picture of Bavaria: the real manifestation as much as the images in people's heads.

Bavaria needs and supports its farmers. The farmers' work shapes the Bavarian cultural landscape with its villages, fields

and meadows. They provide the people with first-class food products and make a valuable contribution to the protection of the environment. For these reasons farmers in Bavaria enjoy the special care and attention of the government.

Even today agriculture in Bavaria has a higher status than in many other parts of Germany. However,

Bayern

goods on offer stretches from different types of cereal to potatoes and vegetables, from fruit for the know all over the world Bavarian beer and the popular dry Franconian wine. There is also dairy and cattle farming with cows, pigs, sheep, goats, horses, poultry and fallow deer on the list of animals to be found on Bavarian farms. 80% of the German carps, for example, come from Bavarian fish

its role in the economy has shrunk drastically over the last decades.

54.2% of Bavaria's land surface is used for agriculture. Yet whereas 1.4 million people lived from agriculture in 1950, this figure was down to 410,000 in 1987. The number of farms with soil of 1 ha of size has sunk from 438,500 to 234,110: at the same time the average size of a farm has risen from 8.7 ha to 14.6.

A big plus point for Bavarian agriculture is its variety. The range of

farms. Bavarian forestry is responsible for woods covering an area of 2.4 million hectares.

Agriculture in Bavaria accounts for 3.3% of the GDP in the Free State and is clearly higher than the 2.2% in the rest of Germany. In 1988 Bavaria's farmers produced 28% of the Federal Republic's total volume of agricultural goods.

The European integrated market will bring great changes in respect to competition in the agricultural industry. New suppliers will force themselves and their products onto the market and anyone wishing to hold a strong position in this changed climate will have to meet the demands with flexibility and determination. For Bavarian farmers this means first and foremost maintaining their standards of quality. Numerous supportive measures have been introduced by the Bavarian government to help farmers continue their training and education, to learn how to implement new technologies and to save costs by working together with colleagues in agricultural marketing.

Moreover, entrepreneurial imagination can help farmers to move into new areas of operation. Some, for example, have extended their services to include work in environmental protection or to offer their premises to those wanting a holiday or recreation on a farm. Other areas such as the exploitation of renewable raw materials or new sources of energy are providing farmers with new perspectives within their chosen profession.

$\mathcal{B}$eer is a special drink. It has been fermenting in world history for 6,000 years. Even the Babylonians had 20 types of beer which, when compared to the 5,000 different types available today in Germany, seems quite modest.

This variety is even more astounding if one considers that "nothing but barley, hops and water are to be used". This is what the oldest food law, the Bavarian Purity Law, insisted on in 1516. Today, as well, brewers are purists whether they like it or not, banning all suspect substances from the tubs and vats. The consumer is grateful to them – German beer is bound to be pure and digestable.

Every fourth brewery in the world is in Bavaria. Today 764

1 The document certifying the Purity Law of 1516.

2 Harvesting hops in the Holledau, the largest hops region in the world.

3 Bottling plant in the Spaten-Franziskaner brewery.

4 Fermenting tanks.

5 Traditional kegs of the Löwenbräu brewery in Munich.

1

Bavarian firms produce their splendid brew for general consumption. Adding it all up together this means 24.9 million hectolitres of beer go into bottles, mugs, glasses and the traditional Keferloher ("stone mugs") every year. In 1989 the 20,000 people employed in the brewing industry recorded a turnover of 4.4 billion DM. A large number of suppliers as well as farmers with hops and yeast live on this industry.

1 *The horses and cart are looked after with great love and care.*

2 *The epitome of Bavarian "Gemütlichkeit": the Oktoberfest in Munich.*

3 *The art of brewing as it once was.*

4 *The brewing plant of the Franziskaner brewery.*

3

4

Anyone who sees beer only in economic terms neglects its deeper meaning. As long ago as the eighteenth century Freiherr von Kreittmayr called beer "Bavaria's Fifth Element". Beer makes you sociable. It loosens the tongue and builds bridges between people of different origins. Moderately consumed it provides a philosophical peacefulness and an inner balance, a tolerant calm which distinguishes the charm of the "liberalitas bavariae".

123

5 *Old "Sudkessel" (Spaten-Franzis-kaner brewery).*

6 *One of the most modern brewing plants in the world. The Hof-bräu brewery in Munich.*

5

6

It is an economic truism that a healthy economic structure is characterized by variety. When different firms of different sizes fight for a share of the market, then potential for innovation and quality is the order of the day and every firm is forced to go on the offensive. The rule that applies to the whole economy applies to the individual company, too: anyone who does not want to be better, stops being good.

The importance of a "mixed structure" of small and large firms was recognized in Bavaria early on as were the political and economic measures to promote it. The magic word for small and medium-sized firms here is Mittelstand, a difficult concept to describe as it covers firms with 200 or 3,000 staff. But it is exactly this fact – that there is a wide spectrum of companies not all lumped together – which signifies a healthy variety.

In order to keep this variety the Bavarian government put support of the Mittelstand high up on its list of priorities early on.

A barrier for many small and

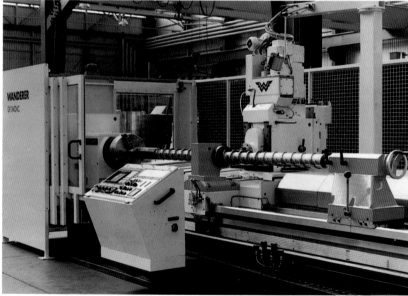

1 *In the world and in Bavaria mechanical engineering is one of the most successful industries in the German economy.*

2 *Flabeg solar reflectors are in use all over the world. The company Flabeg GmbH in Fürth sees its recipe for success in high standards of quality, care for a traditional product range, the development of highly innovative high-tech products and modern marketing methods.*

medium-sized companies is often money. It is here where help from the state is available. Since 1951 the Bavarian institute for financing the Mittelstand has been in charge of this task. Financial support amounts to 3 billion DM annually and includes a host of individual solutions including loans, grants, sureties or participation.

Another barrier is often created by the need for up-to-date technology. In order to make it easier or at all possible for firms to get to know the new technologies, a network of transfer technology offices and user centres were set up throughout Bavaria.

The success of these measures can be seen by the great many technical innovations which originate in Mittelstand firms.

Bavarian firms invest most in terms of research and development. A policy which makes use of company resources in this way – and supported by the state – makes sense economically. Research has shown the connection between investment in research and development and the growth rate of a company. With their wil-

3 *Spraying on a layer of silver in Flabeg's.*

4/5 *Since the 1960s the firm SDS has been working in relay technology and was later able to break through onto the inter-* *national market. From the very beginning SDS collaborated with the Japanese company Matsushita.*

lingness to lend venture capital for establishing companies or for other projects, banks and other credit institutions play their part in giving this development the support it needs.

Many firms in mechanical engineering, electrical engineering, the supply industry for car manufacturers or even the building industry have made a virtue out of being medium-sized. Flexible and ready to adapt, they are in a better position to fill a niche, comply with an individual customer's wish or produce a product to special requirements. Flexibility and speed when developing user-specific solutions guarantee success. The picture shows a Lasco spindle press and the parts it produces than giant enterprises also operating in the same field.

The history of the Bavarian economy is rich in examples of firms which have worked their way up from the smallest beginnings to large companies with thousands of staff, listed on the stock markets and with offices all around the world.

The largest porcelain manufactu-

1/2 *The firm Lasco in Coburg is one of the oldest and experienced companies in the world for forming technology.*

3/4 *A typical example of colaboration of the Mittelstand with other companies is the car manufacturing industry*

Brose Fahrzeugteile has specialized on window winders, seat adjustments and door locks. It is one of the European leaders in this branch.

2

rer in the world, Hutschenreuther AG, with headquarters in Selb, Upper Franconia, is a perfect example. Founded 175 years ago it started to consolidate its market position after the Second World War. Today it has a staff of 6,000 in fourteen plants. Commitments abroad and diversification into areas such as high-performance ceramics and catalytic convertors complete the profile of the company.

127

With so many success stories the idea of a "corporate culture" always has to play a decisive part. Although this concept has be-

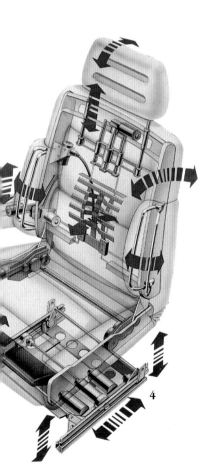

4

3

come increasingly popular over the last few years as something new, companies like Hutschenreuther, Rosenthal or Rodenstock have been practising it for a long time.

Another example of a successful Bavarian company is Schöninger in Munich. It can look back at a 100-year old history of making glass cabinets, museum fittings and dividing walls. Handicraft and technical perfection coupled with a critical view of the present both artistically and culturally have made the company one of

the market leaders in Germany. In this case specialisation, a consistent updating of the necessary skills combined with the ability to work out convincing individual solutions has brought rewards.

2

1-3 Hutschenreuther is not only working in the field of "table and living culture", it is also active in technical ceramics.

3

Bayern

4-7 *Whether it is jewellery or hats, technical equipment in the Deutsches Museum (picture 6) or archaeological findings: Schöninger glass cabinets display the exponents in line with their function and design.*

1 *There's a long way from the first drawings to . . .*

2 *. . . the finished product.*

3 *Incorporating the latest insights: BMW's Research and Engineering Centre.*

4 *The most modern production plants guarantee quality "made in Bavaria".*

3

espite producing less than the services in terms of gross domestic product, industry is still the most important part of the economy. Different branches of industry together reach a turnover of 250 billion DM per year giving work to almost 1.4 million people. Top of the list is the production of capital goods, especially the electronic industry and the car manufacturing industry. Two gems of the German car industry, BMW and Audi, are located in Bavaria. Both enterprises enjoy a worldwide reputation of producing innovative car technology of the highest technical standards. These standards can only be maintained by investing large amounts of money into research and development. The cars are manufactured in highly modern production plants and under constant quality control checks giving new impulses to the car manufacturing technology as a whole.

4

2

Both companies pay special attention to increasing the active and passive security in their cars. Crash tests which show the behaviour of a vehicle in an accident situation are commonplace today. Of equal importance is the search for new production materials which are above all not damaging to the environment. Attempts so far have tried to raise the percentage of materials used in a car which can be recycled. As well as optimising the use of petrol-based engines, large car manufacturers have also been investigating other energy sources. Cars with a combination of petrol-driven and electricty-driven engines have already been developed.

Another possibility might be found by using hydrogen. On the

1 Safety in test: An Audi crash test where the steering wheel retracts.

2-5 Looking for ways of powering motors. Electric and hydrogen-driven engines from Audi (2+5) and BMW (3+4).

6

7

goods vehicle sector Bavaria can be proud of some illustrious names. NEOPLAN in Lower Bavarian Pilsting and MAN supply the international market with buses. Furthermore MAN is able to build enormous engines – for a ship for example. One of the main aims when producing buses is to reduce pollution and noise levels.

6 *Testing the wheel balance at BMW.*

7 *City bus from MAN.*

8 *Inside of an Audi.*

133

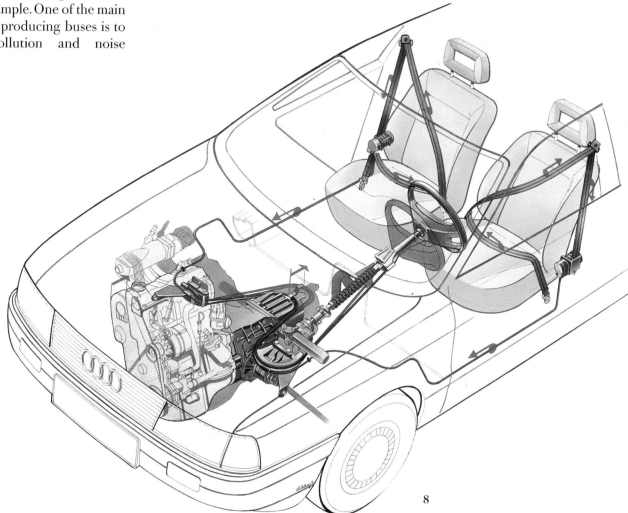

8

1-3 *Ball-bearing technolgy at the firms FAG Kugelfischer and SKF.*

4 *Layers for the production of solar cells and high-temperature supra conductors must be extremely thin and clean.*

5 *Fitting resistors on circuit boards at Rohde & Schwarz.*

Bayern

Numerous products developed and produced in Bavaria are highly regarded and extremely successful on the international market. In many sectors Bavarian companies are among the market leaders. Some of the companies located in Bavaria are AEG, Audi, BMW, FAG Kugelfischer, Fichtel & Sachs, Hutschenreuther, Krauss-Maffei, the headquarters of MAN, MBB, Osram, Rodenstock, Rohde & Schwarz, Rosenthal, Siemens, SKF, Süd-Chemie, and Wacker Chemie. Certain sections of industry have a special emphasis in particular regions within Bavaria. The anti-friction bearing industry has been centred in the Lower Franconian town of Schweinfurt, for example, for 100 years. FAG Kugelfischer and SKF are two internationally renown specialists whose influence goes well beyond the town and even the region. Ball and anti-friction bearings of all shapes and sizes represent the main part of the companies' production but they have long diversified into other sectors. Along with Fichtel & Sachs AG the three firms are important suppliers to the car manufacturing industry.

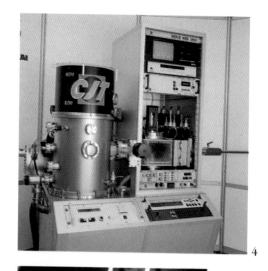

4

5

2

3

Chemicals are part and parcel of modern life. In buildings, paints or sprays. Chemicals are all around us. As time passes the uses chemicals are put to increase with more attention being paid to aspects of ecology and energy. A pamphlet from Wacker Chemie summarises the developments in this century like this: "From the carbide lamp to the microchip". Today silicon of the purest kind is vital for the production of semiconductors. In searching for alternative forms of energy we will also be required to use chemicals. On the wing surfaces of Solair 1, for instance, the solar cells were embedded in transparent silicon rubber.

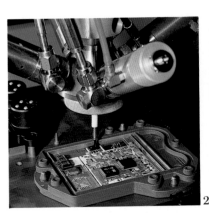

2

1

1 *Pure silicon in the form of poly-crystalline and single-crystalline sticks, disks, polished disks and disks in a special packing device.*

2 *Imperative for the electronics industry: silicon products from Wacker-Chemie.*

3 _Environmental
protection at
Wacker-
Chemie, Burg-
hausen.
Clearing slud-
ge from the
sewage._

3

unich and the surrounding areas represents the fourth largest centre of the electronics industry of the world. The 4 megabit chip, which plays such an important role in the autonomy of the European information technology industry, is produced here. Siemens, one of the world's leading companies in this field, is located in Munich. Countless software producers have branches here, too. About 650 firms are working in the software industry throughout Bavaria. In autumn 1990 the new Siemens-Nixdorf-Informationsysteme AG was officially founded under the motto "Synergy at Work". The new company specializes in PC technology, interactive software, professional systems and integrated office communication.

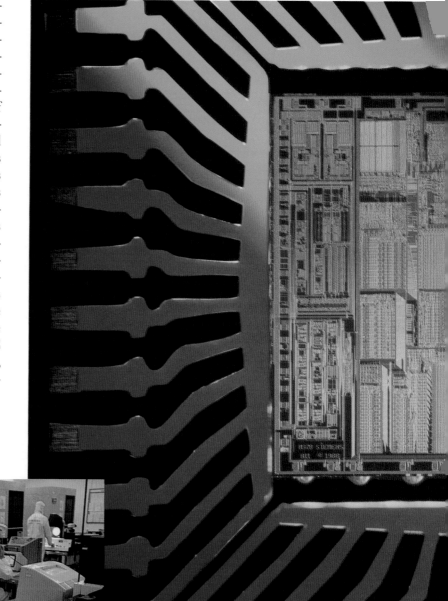

1 *Microchips made in Bavaria are among the best in the world. The 1 megabit chip production at the Siemens plant in Regensburg.*

2 *An example of Siemens' complete ISDN chip series.*

1

3 *The 4 megabit memory contains 8 million elements on one square centimetre. About 250 typed pages can be stored on it.*

4 *The polymerisation process developed by Siemens is being used in the development of the semiconductor switch of the future. The fluorescent light appears when polymerising the plastic layer on the chip.*

hose sectors of the economy and industry which will dominate the future are to be found in Bavaria. Light industry, research institutes and high-tech companies are particularly common here. At the same time, these firms form a background to the different service industries. A colourful and exciting mixture of the most varied suppliers of services has come together in Munich and the surrounding areas creating a unique innovative climate, a critical mass of imagination. These technical, creative minds are developing ideas for the future, for the next millennium. It is not by chance that Munich is Germany's software centre. Most international suppliers of computer programs have their offices there.

The largest German management consultancy firm, Roland Berger, coordinates its international operation in Munich. Other internationally renown companies such as McKinsey, the Boston Consulting Group or the Swiss quality assurance company Qualicon have

offices in and near Munich. The third largest German stock exchange is situated in the capital city and all the important banks have branches in Munich as do 114 credit institutes and 35 foreign banks.

Those who produce and offer services want to inform the rest of the world. The countless advertising and PR agencies which spread their clients' message throughout the world illuminate a further aspect of the service industries. Many of the best and most informative German advertisements are produced in or near Munich.

More than anything else, however, Munich is the centre of the insurance industry. Europe's largest insurance company, Allianz AG, as well as the largest reinsurance company in the world, Munich Re, with business contacts in over 140 countries around the world, have their headquarters in Munich. In addition, Europe's largest legal insurers, the largest German mutual insurance company and numerous smaller firms – in total 190 – are located in Munich.

A special service industry is the ADAC, Germany's national car association. Its headquarters are to be found in Munich and it is from here that the breakdown vehicles and many other services on offer to the 10 million members are coordinated.

2

1 *View of the five-floors belonging to the Amadeus computer centre near Munich's new airport. From here 300 staff are responsible for international reservations in air travel.*

2/3 *The German car club (ADAC) offers its members a service network both nationally and internationally.*

4 *The Bavarian state's bank is the Bayerische Landesbank in Munich.*

4

Bavaria's development from an agricultural state to one of the most active and attractive economic areas in Europe was accompanied by solid financial policies. Concentrated efforts from financial organisations and state institutes were required to make available the means for the enormous investment and modernisation programmes.

With the service industries' share in the the success story of the Bavarian economy growing, the role of the banks has become increasingly important. The integrated market is a real challenge for financial institutions. In order to consolidate and extend Bavaria's lead in key areas of technology, venture capital will need to be made available more readily in future. To do this cooperation between state and banks will also be necessary.

The Free State of Bavaria's bank is the Bayerische Landesbank (BLB), which is also the central bank for the Bavarian savings banks. As one of Germany's leading banks it offers a comprehensive banking service including branches in all the important economic and financial areas of the world. The BLB has a complete range of financial services available to any firm whatever the size

may be. Increasingly small and medium-sized firms are having to deal with international money transactions and need to acquire the knowledge to do so. If you are buying and financing property the BLB is ready to assist you.

From an economic point of view providing individual strategies for the private investor is killing two birds with one stone. First

the capital can be used to finance investment projects and second, an increase in credit means more purchasing power and therefore more consumption.

Apart from in its economic and financial activites the BLB perceives its responsibility within society in another way. Since 1982 when its new premises were completed the BLB has had its own gallery where every month new exhibitions have been shown. Bavarian art and above all contemporary artists or those who have been neglected are the most supported ones.

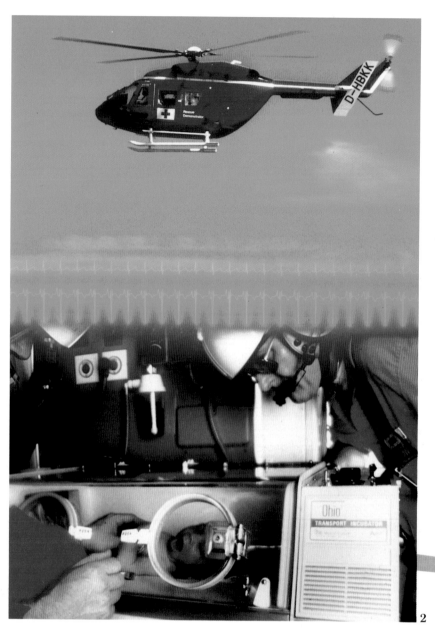

2

The Bavarian state cares for its citizens' health in two main ways: by providing preventive measures and medical treatment. Bavaria has introduced countless projects in the past. Information about diet, medical check-ups for mothers-to-be, advice for parents, check-ups for children, young people and employees at work as well as programmes for the early recognition of cancer. These are just some of services available to citizens in Bavaria. If the worst comes to the worst the ambulance service and hospitals work closely together. Investments in

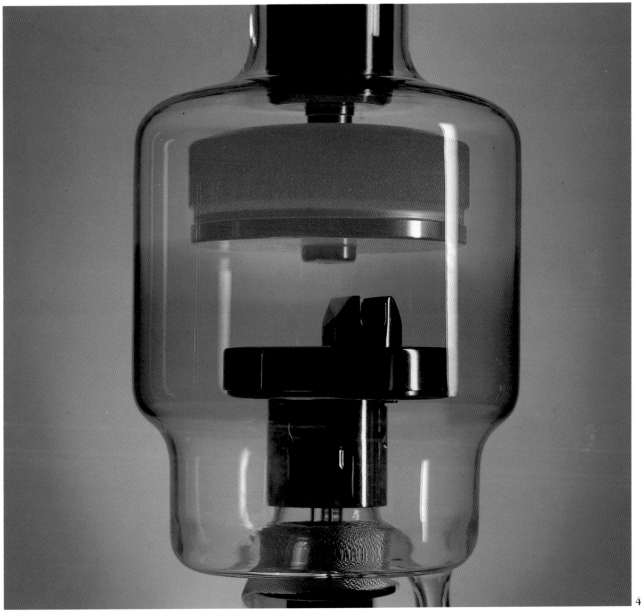

4

1 _The hospital in
Großhadern in
Munich contains
some of the most
modern medical
equipment avail-
able. In fact,
Bavaria leads
Europe in the the
field of cardiology._

2 _A well-organized
emergency service
works in close
cooperation with
hospitals._

3 _The company
Dr. Mach is
among the
leading
manufacturers
of operating
theatre lights._

4 _A CT x-ray
tube produced
by Siemens._

Bayern

Bavarian hospitals are among the highest ones in Germany. The most modern medical technology is now increasingly available including computer tomograpahy and apparatus for destroying kidney, bladder and gall stones. Bavarian hospitals have been particularly successful in the field of transplant surgery and heart surgery. The first German heart centre was established in Bavaria.

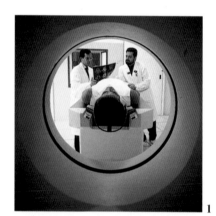

1

2

1 *New perspectives in computer tomography. Somatom Plus from Siemens.*

2 *With the aid of an MBB litho-Las kidney, bladder or gall stones which are difficult to reach can easily be destroyed.*

Bayern

A number of Bavarian companies including MBB, Siemens and Dornier have been extremely successful in the field of medical technology, playing a significant role in the development of new technologies in areas such as lasers, scanner diagnosis and tomography.

3 *Siemens is also active in the field of medical technology. One of the projects they are working on is the development of dosage pumps which are controlled by glucose sensors.*

4 *The mobile scanner diagnosis apparatus AI 300 is considered one of the most advanced products in this field.*

1 Developed by
MBB for the
People's
Republic of
China. The
news satellite
DFH 3.

2 Launch of an
Ariane rocket
in Kourou,
French
Guyana.

3 Control room
at the space
centre in
Oberpfaffen-
hofen.

1

In 1990 the German aviation and space industry was restructured. The companies MTU, Telefunken Systemtechnik, Dornier and Messerschmitt-Bölkow-Blohm, grouped together under German Aerospace (DASA) which is itself a subsidiary of Daimler Benz AG, are actively involved in space research and manufacturing. All these companies are located in or near Munich. The importance and competitiveness of the German aviation and space industry has increased due to this concentration of technological know-how and financial stength. For a long time Munich and the surrounding areas have been a European centre for this technology. Many parts of the Airbus are being developed here. The airbus companies' order books are full and as such justification that the concept of the Airbus is right. Countless other projects for the civil and military aviation industries have taken shape on Bavarian drawing boards and test airfields.

The German research centre for space and aviation (DLR) in Oberpfaffenhofen plays a key role in European space techno-

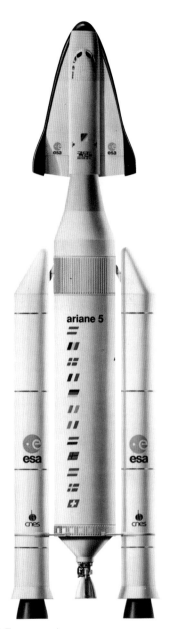

4 *A European project with Bavarian participation. Ariane 5.*

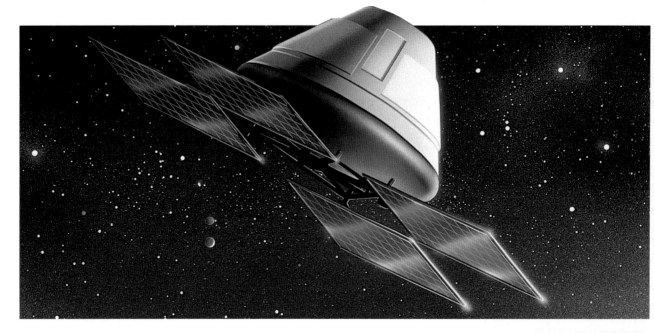

logy. This is where the launches of the European rocket Ariane with its highly sensitive "electronic eyes" are monitored.

The work carried out there includes extremely costly interdisciplinary research projects as well as test and simulation flights. There is also a centre for space automation and space cybernetics.

An area of research which affects us all is climatology. With the aid of a cloud radar new insights can be gained into the structure of weather fronts and the damage to the environment.

One part of the MAN group, Technologie AG in Augsburg, produces essential components for the European rocket Ariane. Engineers at MAN developed a new process for the production of the boosters which hold the fuel to power the rocket. Two tanks are required to transport the rocket into space. The boosters' statistics are impressive. Each one weighs 20 tonnes and measures 25 metres in length and yet it is manufactured to within a thousandth of a millimetre.

1 *The reuseable Ariane-compatible payload capsule CARIANE: an idea for the future.*

2 *MAN develops and manufactures reflectors for radiotelescopes with extreme precision and thermostability*

3 *This radar's job is to investigate what determines our climate. The German research centre for space and aviation in Oberpfaffenhofen hopes to gain information about air pollution, too.*

4 *Important Airbus components are manufactured in Bavaria.*

5 *MAN erected an automised production site covering 10,000 square metres for the manufacture of the booster tanks for Ariane 5.*

6 *MBB's helicopters are the Bavarian aviaton industry's number one in export.*

154

1 *The European*
   space station
   COLOMBUS. This
   computer picture
   shows the
   rendezvous of
   HERMES and a
   free-flying
   laboratory. MBB
   is involved in this
   European project.

2 *The European*
   space glider
   HERMES.

3 *Within the*
   SÄNGER project
   MBB developed
   this engine which
   was driven by
   liquid hydrogen –
   a first in Europe.

4 *A model of the*
   reuseable space
   transporter
   SÄNGER.

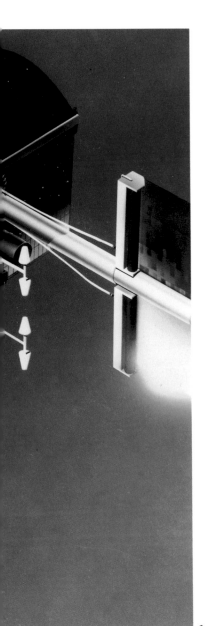

While Adraine sends satellite after satellite into orbit, projects of the next generation are taking shape. The first manned European space glider "Hermes" is one of the spectacular projects for the future as is the reuseable space glider "Sänger II" which will serve both as a supersonic aircraft and as a transporter of satellites. The research module "Colombus" is conceived in such a way that it can link up to an American space station.

It would be a prejudice to think that the aviation and space industries are a domain for giants and the large concerns only. Even in this sector of industry the mixed structure of the Bavarian economy has its part to play. A multitude of suppliers have acquired a highly specialized knowledge of how to construct satellite components, for example. Today there is hardly a space craft, whether American or European, not carrying a Bavarian component into space.

155

1

2

3

4

1 *The world's
first pocket
watch by Peter
Henlein
(1480-1542).*

2 *Zeiss refractor
in the German
Museum.*

Bayern

- the first document in German, the Abrogans (around 770)
- the first German observatory (around 1471)
- the first German globe (around 1500)
- the world's first watch (1511)
- the first German country almanac (1513)
- the world's first Botanic society (1790)
- the first electric telegraph (1809)
- the first German stenograph (1834)
- the first German railway from Nuremberg to Fürth (1835)
- the first German stamp, the "schwarze Einser" (1849)
- the first chain system on a bicycle (1853)
- the first German industrial exhibition (1854)
- the world's first diesel engine (1893)
- the world's first school for church music (1874)
- the first hub for bicycles (1900)
- the first oral vaccination for polio
- the first x-ray examination in the Federal Republic (1953)
- the first German atomic reactor in Kahl am Main (1956)
- the first eye-test for driving test applicants in the FRG
- the world's first automatic dialling service
- the first German SOS children's village
- the first German eye bank
- the first adult education courses on TV
- the first German research satellite "AZUR"
- the first ministry for state development and the environment in Europe (1970)
- the first German heart centre

1 The new fast train Transrapid 07.

2 Art students practising drawing in Munich's Glypothek.

3 The Auditorium Maximum at the Ludwig-Maximilians University in Munich.

4 Joseph von Fraunhofer (1787-1826) who invented optical instruments and discovered the "Fraunhofersche Linien" (lines) in the sun spectrum.

5 Universal theodolite by Merz, Ützschneider and Fraunhofer was built in Munich around 1830.

Bayern

The innovative strength of Bavaria can been seen in today's research infra-structure which is exemplary even outside Germany. Research is carried out and young scientists trained in 32 higher education establishments.

These are:
- the universities in Augsburg, Bamberg, Bayreuth, Erlangen-Nuremberg, Munich, Passsau, Regengsburg and Würzburg

4

- the technical university in Munich
- the Catholic university in Eichstätt
- the Church universities in Benediktbeuren, Munich and Neuendettelsau
- the state polytechnics in Augsburg, Coburg, Kempten, Landshut, Munich, Nuremberg, Regensburg, Rosenheim, Weihenstephan and Würzburg-Schweinfurt

5

- two endowment polytechnics in Munich and Nuremberg
- the polytechnic for civil servants in Hof
- two Fine Art academies in Munich and Nuremberg
- two colleges for music in Munich and Würzburg
- the television and film college in Munich
- the Federal Armed Forces university in Neubiberg

Apart from these academic institutions three large research establishments are based in Bavaria. The Max-Planck Institute for plasma physics in Garching, the Society for Environmental and Ray Research in Neuherberg and the German Research and Test Institute for Space and Aviation with their premises in Oberpfaffenhofen. The Fraunhofer Gesellschaft is also in charge of 8, the Max-Planck-Gesellschaft 13 further facilities within Bavaria. Other research establishments are maintained by the Free State, some independently and others in collaboration with other Federal states or with the German Research Association.

Bavaria has to thank the Ministry for Research and Technology for

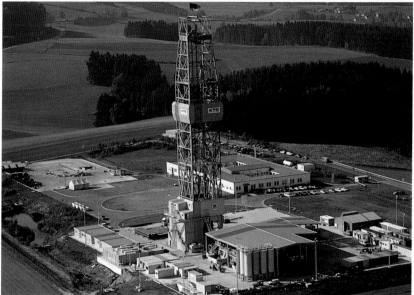

1 An experiment in nuclear fusion, ASDEX Upgrade, in its original stages.

2 The place in Windisch-eschenbach where the deep drilling project is taking place.

3

another world record. In Windischeschenbach, Upper Palatinate, with a population of 6,500 people live, the deepest hole in the earth is being drilled. It is to end 10 to 14 kilometres in the centre of the earth and will hopefully lead to new insights into the geo sciences, including the use of the earth's heat as a source of energy. One of the important establishments in Bavaria is, for example, the Max Planck Institute for extra-terrestial physics in Garching. Together with British and American establishments they have developed

161

4

5

3 *The Max Planck Institute for plasma physics.*

4 *At the Institute for Environmental and Ray Research (GSF) samples from the environment are stored at −140°C using nitrogen so that they can be analysed later.*

5 *Experiments at the GSF. Determining the rate of metabolism in chemical substances located in the cells of people and animals.*

1 Throughout Bavaria the Max Planck Institute has 13 research establishments.

2 ROSAT ready for take off on the rocket.

3 ROSAT – the sharpest eye in x-ray astronomy. Developed by the Max Planck Institute for extra-terrestial physics.

4 Asterix IV, one of the most powerful laser systems in the world.

5 The Max Planck Institute is always making valuable contributions to basic research.

6 This x-ray detector processes the pictures of cosmic x-ray sources received from the telescope for radio transmission.

the world's largest x-ray satellite, Rosat, which is monitored from the German Institute for Space and Aviation Research in Oberpfaffenhofen. Its telescope transmits spectacular pictures of supernova explosions which have taken place hundreds of years before. The systematic search of the skies for sources of x-rays aims to provide data for a new atlas of the stars.

New findings in laser chemistry from the Max Planck Institute for quantum optics, also located in Garching, are promising. A new photochemical method of producing artificial substances to substitute blood is likely to be of great help. It will mean reducing the risk during transfusions (Aids and hepatitis) and providing enough blood whereever needs cannot be met.

The high-performance Asterix IV is one of the most powerful and versatile lasers in the world and the successor to the first ion laser for plasma experiments. The intensity of its beams is approximately 100 billion greater than that of sunlight.

The innovative skills of Bavarian companies is a testimony to Bavaria's creative potential. Since the mideighties more money has been spent on research and development here than in any other Federal state. Bavarian companies invest 10 billion DM annually in R & D.

A significant slice of this money goes to those companies working in so-called "key technologies". Microelectronics, aviation and space technology, bio and gene technology, high-chem: these are the areas receiving most of the money available for research. The willingness of the economy to invest these sums depends completely on the economic and industrial climate in the region. Bavaria offers excellent conditions.

Spectacular projects like the development of a European 4 megabit chip for the international market is one side of the coin. The other is that technological innovation is not only the domain of large enterprises. Small and medium-sized companies also dominate their special fields worldwide.

Support for Mittelstand firms paved the way early on for a range of companies to be organised on a much broader basis than in other Federal states.

The conditions for a well-balanced economic landscape were able to be created in all branches of industry and in all regions of the State. Even if the great names are to be found in Munich and the surrounding areas, all the

1/2 Detailed pictures showing the car's behaviour are just as important as extensive tests in stands equipped with the most modern electronics.

3 In its research and engineering centre BMW has drastically shortened the communication channels between research and production. The times for developing a model can therefore be reduced quite considerably.

4 Germany has perhaps the toughest car market in the world. When it comes to improving car safety time and money are of no concern.

Bayern

3

4

1 *Silicon dominates our age. At Wacker Chemie the drawing process is just over. The crystal will be further processed to make chips.*

2 *Investigating the movements of the eye when in front of a screen will enable researchers to make important discoveries about how user friendly and efficient software is.*

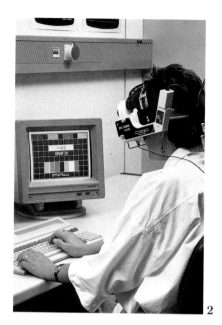

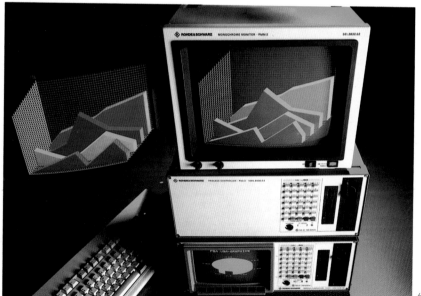

other Bavarian regions offer astonishing potential for future technologies. In the furthest corner of the Upper Palatinate, for example, there is a supplier for NASA and in Neustadt near Coburg you will find the most modern glass fibre leads being manufactured.

Rosenheim in Upper Bavaria is the birthplace of the world's first antenna manufacturer: KATHREIN-Werke KG. Nowadays Kathrein products lead the field in the European antenna industry. The rapid development in technology and research would not be possible without high per-

3/4   *High precision measuring equipment is a speciality of Rohde & Schwarz.*

Other important areas are radio and television technology, radio-location and company radio technology.

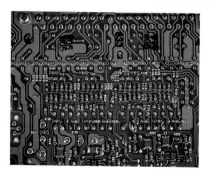

1

formance communication systems. This ranges from large stationary units through satellite and cable to mobile telephone systems in aircraft, trains and cars.

Kathrein's intensive R & D activities have made a significant contribution to the development of modern telecommunications.

Another of Bavaria's strengths is its ability to attract capable human resources. Or putting it another way: to train talented young people and highly qualified specialists who are already here or to get them to move to Bavaria. Other factors, apart from the work itself, contribute to the attractiveness of a firm for a job applicant. A beautiful countryside still intact and a cultural heritage, for example, offer ideal conditions for a worthwhile use of one's leisure time. Quality of life as a factor of production.

2

3

1 The properties of materials are influenced by the smallest traces of foreign substances. Time-consuming analyses are therefore necessary when developing new process technologies or when doing basic research. At Siemens the tunnel microscope can even show up individual atoms.

2 The peak of antenna technology – a Kathrein-system on the Zugspitze, Germany's highest mountain

3 *The Excimer laser offers many opportunities to refine materials.*

4/5 *Theory and practice, basic scintific research and industrial usage complement each other: Wacker Chemie fosters close links to universities.*

6 *In company training courses staff become acquainted with new insights and processes.*

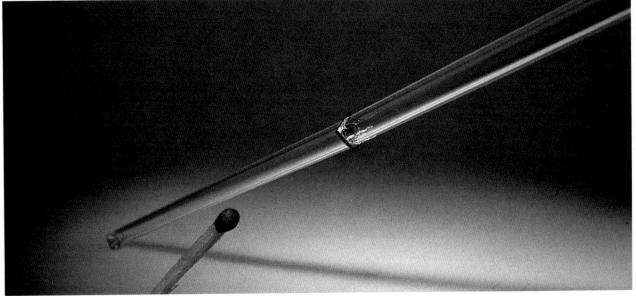

1 *The Ludwig Maximilian University in Munich.*

2 *The Fraunhofer Institute developed the smallest micro-pump in the world. Smaller than a finger nail, the chip with the pump is used in areas such as medicine, chemistry, optics and cybernetics.*

The most pioneering research results are useless unless industry gets to hear about them. Bavaria has therefore developed a range of measures to promote communication betwen universities, institutes and research establishments and business. User centres and technology transfer offices such as the East and West Bavarian Technolgy Centre (OTTI and WETTI) in Regensburg and Nördlingen arrange contacts and inform companies about the possibilities of cooperation and licensing partners.

Companies, too, are actively encouraging a dialogue with universities. BMW, for example, is running a competition throughout Europe, Scientific Award 1991, aimed at young people in tertiary education studying engineering or natural sciences.

The services of the Fraunhofer Society are located at the interface between research and industrial practice. The activities of the 37 institutes in Germany, 8 of which are in Bavaria, are coordinated from the headquarters in Munich.

The Fraunhofer Society carries out research on request in areas such as microelectronics, information technology, production automation, process engineering as well as in health and the environment.

A special programme has been set up to support small and medium-sized companies with a staff of no more than 3,000 to make it easier for them to catch up with the latest technology.

A hotbed for new technolgy is the European Patent Office which has been situated in Munich opposite the German museum on

4

171

3

3 *Quality testing of a wafer for integrated circuits at the Fraunhofer Institute in Erlangen.*

4 *The east Bavarian technology transfer centre (OTTI) in Regensburg encourages dialogue between science and business.*

the opposite bank of the Isar since 1978. After 10 years of existence the Patent Office had been 1989 alone 22,558 inventions were patented. Together with the offices in Brussels and Berlin the EPO employs a staff of 3,000 from all member states. With a minimum of bureaucracy, engineers, research establishments and companies have the possibility to secure the rights of their inventions in 14 countries within Europe.

Thanks to a modern EDP system, quick access to patent information data can be guaranteed. The effect of all this is far reaching. Investment in research and development is protected, and parallel developments can be avoided. The main aim of the EPO is the

172

1 *All facets of technology are to be found in the German Museum.*

2 *The West Bavarian Technolgy Transfer Institute (WETTI) is not only a centre of information for areas such as microelectronics, the use of computers and automation technology, it is also a competent partner for small and medium-sized firms.*

Bayern

exchange and dissemination of knowledge.

The EPO is a splendid example of effective collaboration between different states. In this instance it is good that the EPO is self financing and does not require public assistance.

3

The European Patent Office is one of the most important "trade centres" for new processes, materials and methods.

4 *The wealth of data can only be exploited properly by having quick access to the requi-red information. The EPO has its data on disks, too.*

4

Bavaria is one of the states in Germany which considers business in a positive way. Bavaria's economic policy supports free enterprise as much as possible, insisting on a balance of companies of different sizes. Business, on the other hand, recognises its social responsibilities and supports matters of public concern. The best example for this is the sponsoring which Bavarian companies are engaged in. With a mix of patronage and public relations they promote sports and art as well as making a great number of events possible in the first place.

Good examples of this are the Hypo Bank with their exhibitions in the Kunsthalle in Munich's city centre, Audi and their commitment to the Munich Philharmoniker, BMW and sport or the activities of the Bayerische Landesbank.

2

1 *Audi in Ingolstadt sponsor the Munich Philharmoniker.*

2 *The Bavarian prime minister Max Streibl visiting an exhibition in the Hypo Bank's Kunsthalle.*

3 *Miro is centre stage. An exhibition the Kunsthalle.*

4 *Generous forms: plastic by Niki de St. Phalle.*

5 *Columbia's art export Botero as guest in the Kunsthalle.*

4

5

roducers of sports articles and car manufacturers traditionally have a close relationship in sponsoring, giving them the chance to show their products being used. Adidas and Puma, rivals and neighbours from Herzogenaurach, both support today's (and tomorrow's) famous sportsmen and women.

Audi and BMW are also involved activley and passively in sponsoring sports events. Both companies are keen for success in motor sport since it is a superb opportunity to test their engineering capabilities and to gain useful experience and insights which can then be used the production of their saloon cars.

1+2 *Steffi Graf and Bayern München. First-class performances with the support of Adidas.*

1

Bayern

3

The KATHREIN-Werke KG in Rosenheim has always been receptive to exciting sports.
The internationally known manufacturer of antenna and telecommunication systems is involved in basketball, fencing, windsurfing, volleyball ... and motorsport.
To name but one example, even in Formula 3 speedway championships you will find Kathrein drivers at the starting-line.

2

3 *The Bavarian car manufacturers Audi and BMW are active and successful in motorsport.*

4 *Kathrein Racing Team member – Klaus Lausch, German Speedway Champion (1990).*

4

radition-conscious and modern is a typical Bavarian symbiosis. This combination is important when it comes to protecting the environment. Quality of life without an environment which is natural and intact is unthinkable. Bavaria's countryside is full of charming scenes and this fact led to the Free State reacting earlier than others to the demands of the environment. As early as in 1970 Bavaria established the Ministry for Regional Development and the Environment – the first of its kind in Europe. Another milestone was the inclusion into the Bavarian constitution of environmental protection as one of the state's responsibilities. In article 141 the Free state, the communities and other public institutions pledge to "protect air, ground and water as natural, fundamental life-giving elements and to maintain the efficiency of nature's balance and constantly to improve it."

A great many individual laws define in practice the meaning of protecting the environment – for example.

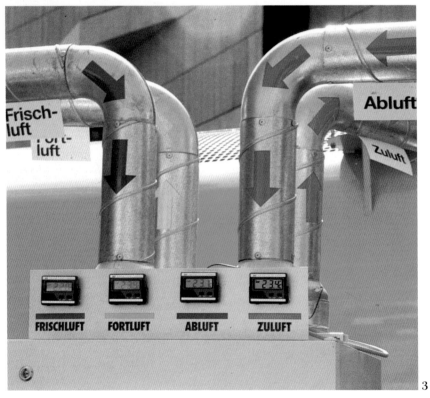

1 _The solar cells on the wings of the solar plane "Solair 1" are embedded in Wacker silicon rubber._

2 _The Munich eco-solar house was built in line with the most recent findings from the acquisition of solar energy._

3 _Apparatus for producing ventilation and heat._

4 _Alternative forms of energy: AEROMAN, a wind power station produced by MAN, located in the wind park on Porto Santo (Madeira)._

2

1-3 *In view of its size the sewerage system around Chiemsee is considered to be the "ecological event of the century".*

4/5 *Recycling has a future. We cannot continue to overexploit the raw materials we have on our planet.*

Bayern

has been updated with more attention being paid to towns and cities. The capital, Munich, has set a good example by bringing out an "environment atlas" which for the first time presents a comprehensive picture of the environmental situation in Munich, from the use of land, to noise reduction, helicopter landing sites and areas of green.

A further example of the effort Bavaria is putting into environment protection is the 1988 programme for the protection of species and biotopes. Handbooks have been written for each district in the State giving information about the animal and plant world as well as the biotopes and outling the measures which need to be taken. In the long run the intention is to create a system of intertwined biotope surfaces, the so-called "biotope integration system". With the help of a citizen information service Bavaria is also breaking new ground. Through the telecommunication system Btx the Ministry for Environmental Protection offers a comprehensive information programme. The latest figures on radiation protection are transmit-

the prevention of water pollution or waste management. Taken everything together Bavaria has the most advanced environmental protection laws in Europe. Within its borders there are 400 nature reserves with a total area of approximately 130,000 hectares.

As long ago as 1974/5, Bavaria as first German state, began to register all its ecologically valuable areas. Since 1985 this data

ted to Btx screens as are gamma doses recorded at 30 measuring stations throughout Bavarian and information about nuclear establishments. Every citizen can use the Btx system to access comprehensive information about keeping the air clean. 38 stations measuring the cleanliness of the air are used to provide this data. The readings for sulphur dioxide, carbon monoxide, nitrogen oxide, ozone and dust can be obtained from a 24-hour service.

Bavaria, a country of mountains, rivers and lakes, made an early start in terms of the prevention of water pollution, too. Countless lakes, such as Tegernsee or Ammersee, are surrounded by sewerage systems. Due to its size and the technical difficulties encountered the sewerage system around Chiemsee, one of the most charming Upper Bavarian lakes, is considered to be "the ecological event of the century". The construction work, begun on 24 November 1989, did indeed set new standards. Within four years 28 kilometres of pipes are to be laid in the lake and 32 on land. In addition these are numerous pumping stations, a high-

ly advanced purification plant and the local sewerage systems for the communities still without proper sanitation facilities amounting to costs of almost half a billion DM.

The results, however, are worth considering. With the new system no sewage from the local community finds its way into the lake. Hopes that Chiemsee will be as clean as it was before industrialisation are soon to be justified. These efforts would all be in vain if sewage from other quarters were to end up in the lake. For that reason the rivers leading

1 Munich's environment atlas offers its citizens reliable figures and dates on all aspects of the environment. Here an walk-round exhibition.

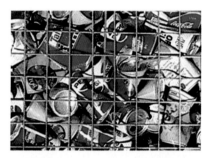

2/3 Waste recycling means that now every individual can contribute to the protection of the environment.

from Chiemsee have also been fitted with modern purification plants.

Bavaria has been consistent in its attempts to reconcile ecology with the economy. Legal requirements and improvements from industry supported with high investment complement each other. Public institutions and business met round the discussion table early on to work out sound concepts for the protection of the environment based on a market economy. An example: The Society for Special Waste Management (GSB). As long ago as the early Seventies the Free State of Bavaria together with leading community groups and business worked out a system for the disposal of special waste to be implemented throughout Bavaria. It was not only the first of its kind then, it can still be considered exemplary today. Since its establishment the GSB has utilized and disposed of 3 million tonnes of special waste without harming the environment.

In the conurbations one subject is especially controversial – the traffic situation. In the north of Munich, under the title "Cooperative Traffic Management", a pilot project is being developed in which BMW is to a large extent involved. New technical and organisational developments are to contribute to make individual and public transport work hand in hand. An optimal use of data, a deliberate control of the traffic flow, an increase in the attractiveness of local public transport will contribute to relieving the city centres of traffic.

183

4 _Environment Day in Munich, 1990. A multitude of creative ideas in ecology including a solar-powered merry-go-round astounded visitors._

5 _The head of Munich's Department of Environment, Dr. Rüdiger Schweikl, talking to Bavarian Radio._

6 _"Ökologius" embodies the possibilities which exist for using alternative energies._

7 _The official signet of Munich's environment atlas links the symbol of the city, the "Münchner Kindl", with the colour-signs for air, water, soil, energie, noise and refuse._

Active environmental protection has other advantages for Bavaria and its businesses. A clean environment and a eco-system which is intact are increasingly having a positive effect on company location in towns and cities. Post-industrial firms and service industries are more likely to settle in attractive areas where there is a charming surrounding countryside. Quality of life and leisure time value are the key ideas here. Both factors will undoubtedly increase in significance when it comes to choosing a site location. For companies the real advantage is in personnel, however, particularly highly-qualified workers or those in upper management. In front of Munich's front door, for example, you can find the Upper Bavarian lakes and the Alps; countless opportunities for sport and recreation entice the people out into the countryside; Vienna, Zurich, Milan and Venice can be reached by train or car within a frew hours. Nobody is surprised to learn that Munich is Germany's most popular city and the one where the majority of citizens would like to live.

1 Keeping nature intact ...

2 ... is an obligation we have to the generations that follow.

Bayern

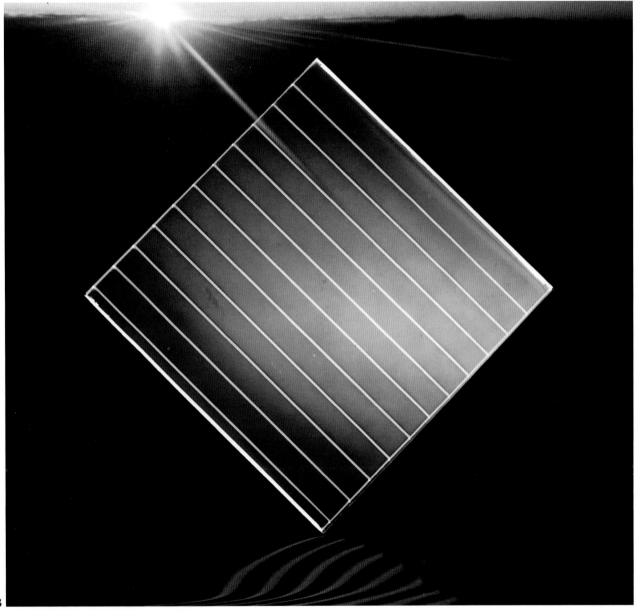

3 *Two aspects of environmental protection. An increased use of solar energy . . .*

4 *. . . and the development of ideas to relieve cities of traffic.*

6

An Economic Area
with a Future

avaria is well equipped for the European integrated market with its strongly export-oriented economy. In the list of the world's trading nations Bavaria ranks sixteenth. Its exports amount to those of Spain and Portugal together. In 1989 exports came to over 100 billion DM. Against this Bavaria imported goods worth of 75 billion DM. As one of the first states in Germany after 1945

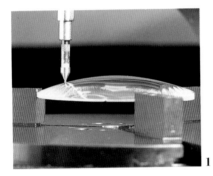

Bavaria began to make economic contact with foreign countries. Today groups of Bavarian companies together with the Bavarian Ministry for Economics and Transport operate in the international arena. At exhibitions and trade fairs they speak out in favour of a strong Mittelstand, for high-tech and for quality "made in Bavaria".

For a number of reasons Bavaria

can look confidently into the future. For one thing after the revolutions in Eastern Europe it has now regained its traditional position at the heart of Europe. Also the structure of the Bavarian economy promises above-average growth in most areas. Electronic engineering, optics, precision engineering, mechanical engineering, automobile production, the wood, paper and printing industries – these branches will have the least problems adapting to an open market.

1-3 *Innovative products of reliable quality guarantees Bavarian industry its high exports.*

4 *Bavaria presents itself throughout the world: at the Saudi Medicare in Riyadh, Saudi Arabia, head of exhibition and trade fairs department Dieter Würl from the Bavarian Ministry for Economics and Transport, talks to the Kingdom of Saudia Arabia's deputy minister for health, Dr. Abdulrahman Al-Sweilam.*

5 *At the Tokyo Toy Show.*

6 *Minister for Economics August Lang and permanent secretary Hanns-Martin Jepsen in Budapest.*

7 *The Minister for Economics and Transport, August Lang, at the Bavarian economic conference in Budapest.*

8 *At the Bavarian economic conference in Prague. The prime minister Max Streibl is in the middle.*

Trade fairs are essential for business contacts. They are an opportunity for personal discussions on an international level, the chance to show new and spectacular products and are quite simply a change of scene. More than that, fairs are an important economic factor.

191

1

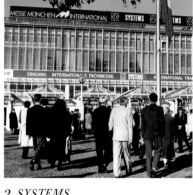

2

1 *An overview of Munich's trade fair complex showing the building machinery fair BAUMA. (Photo release: Upper Bavarian government G30/13144).*

2 *SYSTEMS attracts EDP specialists from all over the globe to Munich.*

The turnover in Bavaria from trade fairs amounted to 2.6 billion DM in 1989 with 17,600 jobs depending directly or indirectly on them. The state also benefits from them. Annual tax revenue is around 120 million DM. Munich and Nuremberg are the two most important sites for trade fairs in Bavaria. Together they attract around 300 million visitors to their stands every year.

Munich is in fact considered one of the most attractive cities in the world for trade fairs. Some of the largest fairs in the world are held here. The ANALYTICA, the waste management fair IFAT with its numerous congresses, SYSTEC, ELECTRONICA and SYSTEMS in the field of electronic engineering, data processing, BAUMA and many others attract top-class specialists to Munich.

The annual toy fair in Nuremberg is a special type of magnet. Munich's ISPO, for sports articles and sports clothes, enjoys great popularity, too. And finally Munich's fashion week (MODE WOCHE), taking place several times a year, presents the latest collections, accessories and designs.

193

Despite retaining its special characteristics and fostering its local customs, Bavaria has remained open-minded. Munich's title as "the capital with a heart" is not least due to the gregariousess of its citizens. This international network has revolutionised our political, economic and cultural life in a way which will have far-reaching consequences.

Only those who today have access to and can use different means of communication will have a say tomorrow. Whoever wants to talk tomorrow about what is going to happen the day after tomorrow, has to do more. He must participate in forming the means, contents, media and messages of communication. Bavaria does this.

Munich is one of the most im-

1 *This is the way the branch of newspaper printing came into being in Bavaria after world war II: The American military government granted the "License Number One" to the "Süddeutsche Zeitung".*

portant media cities in Germany employing 60,000 people. A great many more publishing houses than in any other German city are situated here. Four daily pap-

ers and countless magazines are produced here. After New York Munich is book city number 2 in the world.

In Bavaria 250 papers appear and 3 million are sold every day. More than 1,200 differnt magazines inform and entertain the people. The Bavarian printing industry is particularly powerful with over 2,500 firms. One of the leading manufacturers of printing machines, MAN Roland, is located in Bavaria.

A lively group of private TV and radio stations provide entertainment and information. As long ago as in May 1945 the first radio programmes were broadcasted in post-war Bavaria. In 1954 television entered people's living-rooms. Bayerische Rundfunk (BR) is one of the largest broadcasting stations in Germany. In December 1984 with the passing of a media development law, an essential step was taken to liberalise radio and television in Bavaria. It led the way to open the information market to private suppliers. The Bavarian State Institute for New Media is responsible for coordinating the activities of the private TV and radio stations.

A larger selection of entertainment is based a variety of opinions. The Bavarian government has good arguments when speaking in favour of increasing the range of media in Bavaria.

2

3

2 *MAN Roland is one of the world's leading manufacturers of printing presses.*

3 *The close link between editorial team and production is only one example of the revolution which computers have caused in the media world.*

2

3

More than half of the jobs in the German film industry are to be found within Bavaria, especially in Munich. In the highly modern film studios of the Bavaria Film GmbH in Geiselgasteig, or the "Hollywood on the Isar" as it is sometimes called, films of international standing such as "A Never-ending Story" or "The Boat" were made. At the College for TV and Film young people train to get the qualifications they need to make a career. The status attributes by Bavaria to cinematic art can be gauged by the large number of film festivals which are held here. Since 1980 outstanding productions have been awarded the Bavarian Film Prize. A programme supporting upcoming talented young people is available to those in the film industry.

1 *The satellite Kopernikus transmits radio and TV programmes.*

2/3 *Worldwide cinema successes are produced in the Bavaria film studios near Munich.*

4 *A large number of private TV stations have broadened the range of media available.*

5 *Satellites make it possible. A global network of information has already become reality.*

6 *The German National Post Office's ground radio station near Raisting.*

he sky over Bavaria is blue and white. The horizon which looks into the future is rosy.

Europe's borders are being re-laid – geographically and intellectually as well as economically. After decades of division Germany has been reunited again. In east-European states a market economy is gaining a foothold. The European community is progressing with its policy of integration.

These developments not only correspond to Bavaria's political aims, they put the Free State in the role of a central trading country in the middle of Europe. Goods between east and west and north and south travel to a large extent through Bavaria. Above all Bavaria will become an important trading place for intangible goods, for know-how, patents, new technologies and cultural impulses.

Bavaria can look confidently into the future. The prerequisites are there. A concentrated potential of technological skills, innovative talent, creativity and more than anything else a productive blend of traditional and modern times.

Bayern

With all that, Bavarian politics and Bavarian companies will play a decisive role in shaping the future.

Bavaria has already shown what a part of that future will look like. Highly innovative, key technologies and an environment which is still intact are not contradictions, but mutually dependent. Only the most advanced technology is capable of providing the means to retain nature.

avaria is not an "island of the blessed". We have problems just as others do around the world-only, perhaps fewer. In Bavaria, too, people only "cook with water". Its fate lies in the hands of quite normal people. But people who are aware of their heritage and their traditions.

The prerequisites are good: a concentrated potential of technological skills, innovative talent and creativity.

Together with the advantages of an excellent transport system, sound politics and beautiful countryside, these prerequisites are concentrated in a place which is not only attractive but is also considered to have great prospects for the future. A place at the top where companies find a friendly attitude towards business, where investment is encouraged and where a technological and ecological dynamism can be felt. Nobody knows what tomorrow will bring in Germany's white-and-blue state in the south. To sum up we can look ahead with hope, carried forward by the certainty of leaving our mark somewhere in the future.

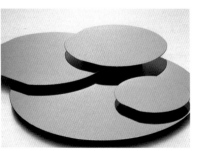

Bayerisches Staatsministerium für
Wirtschaft und Verkehr
Prinzregentenstr. 28, Postfach
8000 München 22
Tel. (0 89) 21 62-01
Fax (0 89) 21 62-27 60

Bayerische Landesanstalt für
Aufbaufinanzierung
Königinstr. 15
8000 München 22
Tel. (0 89) 21 24-0
Fax (0 89) 21 24-4 40

Bundesstelle für Außenhandels-
information (BfAI)
Blaubach 13, Postfach 10 80 07
5000 Köln 1
Tel. (02 21) 20 57-1
Fax (02 21) 20 57-2 12

Bundesamt für Wirtschaft (BAW)
Frankfurter Str. 29-31, Postfach 51 71
6236 Eschborn/Ts.
Tel. (0 61 96) 4 04-1
Fax (0 61 96) 4 04-2 12

DEG – Deutsche Investitions- und
Entwicklungsgesellschaft mbH
Belvederestr. 40, Postfach 45 03 40
5000 Köln 41
Tel. (02 21) 49 86-0
Fax (02 21) 49 86-2 90

Deutsche Gesellschaft
für Technische Zusammenarbeit
(GTZ) GmbH
Dag-Hammarskjöld-Weg 1
Postfach 51 80
6236 Eschborn 1
Tel. (0 61 96) 79-0
Fax (0 61 96) 71 74

HERMES Kreditversicherungs-AG
Friedensallee 254, Postfach 50 07 40
2000 Hamburg 50
Tel. (0 40) 8 87-0
Fax (0 40) 8 87-77 44
Außenstelle:
Arnulfstr. 44, 8000 München 2
Tel. (0 89) 55 15 02-0
Fax (0 89) 55 15 02-66

*Chamber of
Industry and
Commerce in
Munich*

Chambers of Industry and Commerce

Aschaffenburg:
Kerschensteinerstr. 9, Postfach 17
8750 Aschaffenburg
Tel. (0 60 21) 8 80-0
Fax (0 60 21) 8 79 81

Augsburg und Schwaben:
Stettenstr. 1 u. 3, Postfach 10 18 80
8900 Augsburg
Tel. (08 21) 31 62-0
Fax (08 21) 31 62-3 23

Oberfranken:
Bahnhofstr. 25-27, Postfach 10 06 53
8580 Bayreuth
Tel. (09 21) 8 86-0
Fax (09 21) 1 27 78

Coburg:
Schloßplatz 5, Palais Edinburg
Postfach 3 84, 8630 Coburg
Tel. (0 95 61) 77 94
Fax (0 95 61) 9 93 70

Lindau-Bodensee:
Maximilianstr. 1, Postfach 13 65
8990 Lindau/Bodensee
Tel. (0 83 82) 40 94 und 40 95
Fax (0 83 82) 40 57

München und Oberbayern:
Max-Joseph-Str. 2, 8000 München 2
Postfach, 8000 München 34
Tel. (0 89) 51 16-0
Fax (0 89) 51 16-3 06

Nürnberg:
Hauptmarkt 25-27, Post-Abholfach
8500 Nürnberg 106
Tel. (09 11) 13 35-0
Fax (09 11) 13 35-5 00

Niederbayern/Passau:
Nibelungenstr. 15, Postfach 17 27
8390 Passau
Tel. (08 51) 5 07-0
Fax (08 51) 5 07-2 80

Regensburg:
Dr.-Martin-Luther-Str. 12
Postfach 11 03 55, 8400 Regensburg
Tel. (09 41) 56 94-1
Fax (09 41) 56 94-2 79

Würzburg-Schweinfurt:
Mainaustr. 33, Postfach 1 27
8700 Würzburg 1
Tel. (09 31) 41 94-0
Fax (09 31) 41 94-1 00

Handwerkskammer für Oberbayern
Max-Joseph-Str. 4, 8000 München 2
Tel. (0 89) 51 19-0
Fax (0 89) 51 19-2 95

**Handwerkskammer für Mittel-
franken – Exportberatungsstelle
des Bayerischen Handwerks**
Sulzbacher Str. 11, 8500 Nürnberg
Tel. (09 11) 53 09-1
Fax (09 11) 53 09-2 88

**Handwerkskammer für
Oberfranken**
Kerschensteinerstr. 7, 8580 Bayreuth
Tel. (09 21) 9 10-0
Fax (09 21) 9 10-3 09

**Handwerkskammer für
Unterfranken**
Rennwegerring 3, 8700 Würzburg
Tel. (09 31) 3 09 08-0
Fax (09 31) 3 09 08-53

Handwerkskammer für Schwaben
Schmiedberg 4, 8900 Augsburg
Tel. (08 21) 32 59-0
Fax (08 21) 32 59-2 71

Handwerkskammer zu Coburg
Hinterer Floßanger 6, 8630 Coburg
Tel. (0 95 61) 68 04-1
Fax (0 95 61) 6 85 86

**Handwerkskammer Niederbayern-
Oberpfalz**
Ditthornstr. 10, 8400 Regensburg
Tel. (09 41) 79 65-0
Fax (09 41) 79 25 50

**Handwerkskammer Niederbayern-
Oberpfalz**
Nikolastr. 10, 8390 Passau
Tel. (08 51) 53 01-0
Fax (08 51) 5 81 45

**Landesverband der Bayerischen
Industrie e.V.**
Maximiliansplatz 8, 8000 München 2
Tel. (0 89) 59 28 71
Fax (0 89) 59 61 70

**Landesverband des Bayerischen
Groß- und Außenhandels e.V.**
Max-Joseph-Str. 4, 8000 München 2
Tel. (0 89) 55 77 01
Fax (0 89) 59 30 15

**Verband Deutscher Maschinen- und
Anlagenbau e.V. (VDMA)
Landesgruppe Bayern**
Tengstr. 37, 8000 München 40
Tel. (0 89) 2 71 64 64
Fax (0 89) 2 72 29 19

**Zentralverband der Elektro-
technischen Industrie e.V. (ZVEI)
Landesstelle Bayern**
Blumenstr. 6, 8500 Nürnberg
Tel. (09 11) 20 49 16
Fax (09 11) 22 26 19

**Verband der Bayerischen
Spielwaren-Industrie e.V.**
Messezentrum, 8500 Nürnberg 50
Tel. (09 11) 8 66 88
Fax (09 11) 86 83 81

**Verband der Keramischen
Industrie e.V.**
Schillerstr. 1, 8672 Selb
Tel. (0 92 87) 7 90 33
Fax (0 92 87) 7 04 92

**Verein der Bayerischen Chemischen
Industrie e.V.
Landesverband Bayern**
Innstr. 15, 8000 München 80
Tel. (0 89) 9 26 91-0
Fax (0 89) 9 26 91-33

**Verein der Bayerischen Metall-
industrie e.V.**
Brienner Str. 7, 8000 München 2
Tel. (0 89) 2 90 79-0
Fax (0 89) 22 28 51

**Verein der Südbayerischen
Textilindustrie e.V.**
Gewürzmühlstr. 5, 8000 München 22
Tel. (0 89) 29 25 45
Fax (0 89) 39 62 40

**Verband der Nordbayerischen
Textilindustrie e.V.**
Blücherstr. 4, 8670 Hof
Tel. (0 92 81) 99 54-0
Fax (0 92 81) 9 38 68

**Landesfremdenverkehrsverband
Bayern e.V.**
Prinzregentenstr. 18, 8000 München 22
Tel. (0 89) 21 23 97-0
Fax (0 89) 29 35 82

203

Bayern

	Unit	1980	1989	1990
Area	km²	70,546	70,554	70,554
Population (31. 12.)	1,000	10,928	11,221	11,449
females	1,000	5,699	5,800	5,893
males	1,000	5,229	5,421	5,556
age under 15	%	18.1	15.6	15.8
15 to 65	%	66.7	69.3	69.1
65 and over	%	15.2	15.1	15.1
density of population (per km²)	number	155	159	162
aliens	1,000	711	763	856
Turks	%	29.6	29.3	27.5
Jugoslavians	%	18.0	15.7	15.7
Austrians	%	11.3	10.6	10.4
Italians	%	11.9	9.3	9.4
Natural Movement of Population				
births	number	114,451	127,029	136,122
excess of birth over deaths	number	−8,408	5,686	12,396
migration surplus	number	65,464	165,786	215,692
Private Households	1,000	4,286	4,959	4,916
one person household	%	28.9	35.2	34.0
two persons	%	28.1	29.4	29.2
three persons and over	%	43.0	35.4	36.8
Employment	1,000	5,174.7	5,416.2	5,731.4
agriculture and forestry	1,000	523.0	373.8	362.8
manufacturing	1,000	2,331.5	2,268.1	2,412.0
trade and transport	1,000	856.1	897.6	936.4
banking and insurances	1,000	154.8	192.1	206.5
other services	1,000	829.3	1,117.5	1,209.7
public sector	1,000	402.9	470.0	487.6
private households	1,000	77.1	97.1	116.4
Employment-Population Rate (per cent of population)	%	47.5	48.9	50.7
Self-Employment Rate (per cent of employments)	%	10.4	10.0	9.9
Labour Market				
unemployed	1,000	148	266	241
vacancies	1,000	61	55	71
short-time workers	1,000	23	15	10
unemployment rate	%	3.5	5.7	5.1
Gross Domestic Product				
real (at 1980 prices)	bill. DM	249.8	319.5	336.7
per capita	DM	22,916	28,780	29,700
per person employed	DM	51,609	60,570	60,690
at current prices	bill. DM	249.8	405.2	442.3
per capita	DM	22,916	36,510	39,020
per person employed	DM	51,609	76,820	79,720

	Unit	1980	1989	1990
Sector share of gross value added (At current prices)				
agriculture and forestry	%	3.2	2.3	2.3
manufacturing	%	42.7	40.2	40.2
trade and transport	%	15.3	14.3	14.1
banking and insurances	%	5.0	5.4	5.4
other services	%	20.7	26.1	26.4
public sector	%	11.7	10.3	10.1
private households	%	1.4	1.5	1.5
Agriculture and Forestry				
agricultural enterprises	1,000	273	230	224
productive land area	km²	61,003	60,083	59,990
Industry				
business units	number	10,135	9,901	9,892
employed	1,000	1,386	1,401	1,443
sales	mill. DM	183,204	285,460	309,198
foreign sales rate	%	25.7	34.3	32.2
wages and salaries	mill. DM	42,157	63,256	68,797
per person employed	DM	30,425	45,145	47,664
as a percentage of total sales	%	23.0	22.2	22.3
level of skills of male industrial workers	1,000	670	685	709
skilled workers	%	55.0	57.3	56.9
semi-skilled workers	%	37.6	35.3	35.4
unskilled workers	%	7.4	7.4	7.7
investments	mill. DM	8,864	15,143	16,555
per person employed	DM	6,320	11,116	11,693
investments for environmental protection	mill. DM	250.4	467.5	600.8
per person employed	DM	497	831	1,054
Handicrafts (Including industrial crafts)				
business units	1,000	126	134	136
employees	1,000	950	940	960
sales	mill. DM	91,000	123,500	138,000
Construction Industry				
business units	number	11,608	13,840	14,489
employees	1,000	263	226	232
sales	mill. DM	21,664	27,872	30,700
wages and salaries	mill. DM	7,543	8,664	9,420
per person employed	DM	28,670	38,283	40,607
as a percentage of total sales	%	34.8	31.1 (1988)	30.2 (1989)
investments	mill. DM	1,070	899	1,074
per person employed	DM	5,004	5,174	6,300
Building completion				
business units	number	936	1,060	1,123
employees	1,000	38	44	47
sales	mill. DM	2,945	5,095	5,894

Bayern

	Unit	1980	1989	1990
wages and salaries	mill. DM	991	1 622	1 839
per person employed	DM	26,279	36,513	38,823
as a percentage of total sales	%	33.7	31.8	31.2
			(1988)	(1989)
investments	mill. DM	77	120	143
per person employed	DM	1,824	2,606	2,887
Services			(1986)	(1988)
Trade				
business units	number	107,985	113,804	114,990
sales	mill. DM	165,292	198,551	211,994
Transport and Communication				
business units	number	14,946	16,091	17,001
sales	mill. DM	11,296	15,139	17,238
other services				
business units	number	98,003	137,700	153,134
sales	mill. DM	50,239	84,841	104,953
Tourism				
arrivals	1,000	14,441	18,562	20,039
share of foreigners	%	17.9	21.8	22.8
overnight stays	1,000	60,486	70,346	73,771
share of foreigners	%	9.2	12.1	12.6
Foreign Trade				
exports, total	mill. DM	47,179	100,144	100,392
share in world export	%	1.30	1.76	1.85
imports, total	mill. DM	46,973	75,509	83,454
share in world import	%	1.26	1.28	1.47
Public Finances				
expenditure of **federal state**, total	mill. DM	32,870	45,577	48,238
expenditure of communities and municipal corporations	mill. DM	28,236	41,596	43,419
investments per inhabitant				
state	DM	691	814	839
communities	DM	819	988	1,015
Public debt per capita				
state	DM	1,513	2,868	2,940
communities	DM	1,199	1,503	1,530
Cost-of-Living Index				
all private households	1985=100	82.4	104.2	107.0
Wages and Salaries				
workers (industry incl. construction)				
gross monthly income women	DM	1,684	2,373	2,472
men	DM	2,429	3,334	3,473
employees (trade and industry)				
gross monthly income women	DM	2,098	3,029	3,195
men	DM	3,259	4,753	4,957

	Unit	1980	1989	1990
Pupils				
elementary schools	1,000	997	768	793
grammar schools	1,000	330	268	272
secondary schools	1,000	179	121	121
comprehensive schools	1,000	7	8	8
vocational schools	1,000	515	410	400
foreign pupils (all kinds of schools)	1,000	102	123	128
Vocational Training				
trainees, total	1,000	335	281	269
trade and industry	1,000	144	136	133
handicrafts	1,000	152	108	98
liberal professions	1,000	21	24	24
agriculture	1,000	12	6	5
public sector	1,000	7	7	8
Students	1,000	151	242	256
students from abroad	1,000	7	11	12
Consumption of Primary Energy	mill. tonnes of coal equivalent	55.4	(1988) 59.3	(1989) 58.5
oil	%	61.7	50.6	48.0
nuclear energy	%	2.7	20.2	21.8
gas	%	11.9	13.3	14.9
coal	%	11.2	8.1	7.9
hydro-electric power	%	11.7	6.5	6.0
other sources of energy	%	0.8	1.3	1.4
Electric Power Production, total	mill. kWh	41,363	68,916	70,853
thermal	mill. kWh	30,392	57,710	60,182
hydro-electric	mill. kWh	10,971	11,205	10,672
share of nuclear energy	%	10.8	61.1	58.0
Road Network (31. 12.)				
federal motorways	km	1,637	2,037	2,063
federal trunk roads	km	7,217	7,128	7,141
state roads	km	13,627	13,801	13,816
district roads	km	17,036	18,293	18,380
community roads	km	90,000	94,000	93,000
Number of Vehicles (31. 12.)	1,000	5,009	6,734	6,895
cars, total	1,000	4,092	5,553	5,683
with "reduced" pollution	%	–	40.4	49.5
density (per 1,000 inhabitants)	number	374	495	496
density per 1,000 private households	number	951	1,120	1,156
Railroad-Network	km	7,185	6,952	6,907

	Area (1,000 km²)	Population (mill.)	Density of Population (per km²)
Bayern	70.6	11.34	162
Baden-Württemberg	35.8	9.77	273
Berlin	0.88	3.42	3,886
Brandenburg	29.1	2.61	90
Bremen	0.4	0.68	1,700
Hamburg	0.8	1.64	2,050
Hessen	21.1	5.72	271
Mecklenburg-Vorpommern	23.8	1.95	82
Niedersachsen	47.4	7.34	155
Nordrhein-Westfalen	34.1	17.24	506
Rheinland-Pfalz	19.9	3.73	187
Saarland	2.6	1.07	412
Sachsen	18.3	4.84	264
Sachsen-Anhalt	20.1	2.92	143
Schleswig-Holstein	15.7	2.61	412
Thüringen	16.3	2.65	163
Germany	357	79.48	223
Belgium	30.5	10.0	328
Denmark	43.1	5.1	118
France	551.5	56.4	102
United Kingdom	244.1	57.4	235
Greece	132.0	10.1	77
Ireland	70.3	3.5	50
Italy	301.3	57.6	191
Luxembourg	2.6	0.4	154
Netherlands	40.8	14.9	365
Portugal	92.4	10.4	113
Spain	504.8	39.0	77
EC	2,370.3	344.2	145
USA	9,372.6	251.4	27
Japan	377.8	123.5	327

Bayern

List of Illustrations